Angela's Anorexia
The story of my mother

Damian Cooper

First ebook edition: Sydney, 2015.
Publisher: Sydney School of Arts & Humanities
73 Garden St Alexandria 2015 Australia
www.ssoa.com.au
ISBN: 978-09875961-8-5

What follows is a true story. All dates, place names and
events in this memoir are factual. However, in
accordance with the wishes of certain participants, many
names have been changed in order to protect their
privacy

Dedication

This book is principally dedicated to my mother.
The dedication extends to my wife Jasmine and my
daughter Georgia who, above all other things, have
taught me that the unknowable future abounds with
limitless opportunities for happiness.

He is a boy who should have been full of fun but because
I have worked and been in strife, he has suffered most of
his life ...
I see him as a pearly shell.
Angela Cooper (1986)

Acknowledgements

Foremost, I would like to gratefully acknowledge Ken Warren who has always stood by me, giving me his support throughout my life.

This book is based on an earlier first draft written for an Honours course in Narrative and Cultural Studies as part of a Bachelor of Arts degree from Southern Cross University, Lismore. I would like to thank my supervisor, Dr Janie Conway-Herron, for her supervision and support.

I would also like to thank Dr Sharon Dean, for her encouragement after reading my first draft manuscript and later for proofreading the final manuscript. Much appreciation goes to Dr Christine Williams who carried out the editing and shaping of the final memoir. I also appreciate the care that Nick Waters has taken in formatting my manuscript as an ebook, and thank Latif Rabhi, Lounis Boukhezzar and Vernon Song for their website assistance at Sydney School of Arts & Humanities.

For Help with Eating Disorders
If you care for a loved one with an eating disorder, or you or someone you know needs help with an eating disorder, call the Butterfly Foundation helpline
1800 ED HOPE / 1800 33 4673 (FREE) or email
support@thebutterflyfoundation.org.au

For Emergency Help
If you are in an emergency situation or need immediate assistance, you can contact mental health services or emergency services on 000.
If you need to speak to someone urgently call:
Kids Helpline 1800 55 1800 (FREE) or
Lifeline 13 11 14
or Suicide Call Back Service 1300 659 467.

Contents

Chapter 1

The phone call I had been waiting for all my life occurred without my having any knowledge of it. Yet eventually, when the news finally filtered its way down to me, I immediately knew its significance. Sergeant Ross had called out from his demountable office in the corner of the Army motor pool yard, 'Private Cooper, phone call,' These four simple words might have pointed to a great many possibilities. Yet at that very moment, as I stood listlessly on the parade ground, there was not a shred of doubt in my mind that those words meant that my mother had now probably died.

It was early May 1996 and I had been in the Army since my eighteenth birthday in January that year, posted to an old Vietnam War conscripts' training base in Puckapunyal in southern Victoria. I had recently completed my three months of basic training and had moved straight on to do a driver training course, which is how I came to be under the ever-present and watchful eye of Sgt Ross and his many six-wheeled camouflage Land Rovers.

Receiving a phone call on that uncharacter-istically warm and dry Wednesday morning in autumn made me feel even more alienated than usual. The Army is not a place for individuals. As soldiers we shared bedrooms, our showers had no walls, and every task assigned by our superiors – from washing the latrine to assaulting a hill – was done as a team. So to be singled out, to be directed individually to take a phone call, which was a task of relative privacy, could only mean trouble. Immediately, pressure built in my head. I had been bleeding the diesel fuel line of my six-by-six truck with Donaldson, my driving partner, when the sergeant's fog horn voice had reverberated across the parade ground. I immediately felt Donaldson's eyes lock onto me with intrigued confusion, but my head was lowered in the engine bay and I did not meet his gaze as I stood and turned toward Sgt Ross.

I knew that my mother was either dying or already dead. Although my first thought was that she was dead, it did occur to me that she might still 'be dying'. But most likely dead, I thought, since no one would bother to call just to say she was dying – she had already been dying for a long time. No, somehow I knew this was different, I knew this was for real, the moment I had been anticipating all my life, the moment I had imagined, played out in my mind, feared and fantasised about for as long as I could remember. I was determined to savour every bit of it, like a child with a long-awaited ice cream. Having dwelt for so many years on the prospect of how and when my mother would die, I was resolute that I would not let the moment rush by me. So, I put the screwdriver down on the wheel arch, turned my back on Donaldson without a word, secured my slouch-hat on my head and began to march indifferently across the square.

I felt disconnected from my body, not in the way people describe being outside of themselves, looking down. But in a more surreal sense, as if I were a Salvador Dali painting animated into existence and marching to the dull 'clomp clomp' of my standard issue Army boots. As Sgt Ross, exercising a minimum of dialogue, handed me over to a nondescript fellow from battalion headquarters at the wheel of a staff car, I wondered about who might already know the news but wasn't saying anything. I also wondered about who would eventually come to know, thinking about Donaldson and Crawford, and my other mates from basic training. Would they know the truth or would I forever be the guy who one day got a phone call and never came back? The staff car shuttled me all too quickly to Battalion HQ where I encountered perplexed expressions on the faces of soldiers who had never been trained to deal with rogue civilian phone calls. They failed miserably at hiding their sympathy.

Finally, having traversed a warren of partitioned half-wall office spaces where hapless-looking, khaki-clad 'drones' stood about, someone pointed into a private corner office equipped with a door and said, 'There's the phone.' And sure enough, there it was. The young admin officer, having pointed it out as if it was a suspected dirty bomb or a pile of radioactive waste, began to back away. In my invisible bio-hazard suit, I gingerly ventured forth, my movements slow and deliberate and my focus unfaltering as I stared at the displaced phone handset resting on the desk. I heard the door shut behind me, which both startled me and added to my sense of unease as I had never been this alone, physically and emotionally, since the day I had joined the Army. I breathed while Dali continued to paint. I sat down in someone's chair, picked up the receiver and looked at it for a moment. It was a '70s-style receiver with large ear and mouth pieces. It was mustard yellow and it felt very cold.

'Hello?' My voice disappears down into the little black holes of the receiver not knowing where it's going.

'Hello Damian, this is Ian here ...'

'Hi Ian, how are you?' I cut in. The words coming out of my mouth are a reflex revealing nothing of my suspicions and sounding more like I have just been thinking of calling him myself for a casual chat.

'Well, Damian ...' Ian's sober monotone voice descends over my welcoming tone like a grey cloud. 'I'm calling with some bad news about your Mum ...'

'*Bad news you say?*' I want to interject. '*Bad bloody news? You can't be serious!*'

This sarcasm could easily drip from my mouth in an attempt to erect a solid wall of protection around my increasingly vulnerable emotions - but I don't say these words and Ian continues.

'She has taken a bit of a turn for the worse, Damian, and it's not looking good.'

'Okay.'

'She has been very weak for the last week, Damian. Rachel and I have been visiting, and Dr Weedon from the medical centre across the road has been coming over to your Mum's unit each afternoon after work to check on her.'

I say nothing. There is nothing for me to say.

'We knew the end was getting close. The doctor explained that her organs were starting to fail. They were just too depleted from the years of not eating, and he had told us that it wasn't going to be long for your Mum and that there was nothing that could be done. Damian ...?'

He keeps saying my name; he keeps talking about her in the past tense; he just keeps talking yet I seem not to take notice of the importance of what is being said, as if his voice is a recorded message that I have already heard many times before. I am not numb, just feeling my body as hyper-real or dispossessed. I acknowledge my responses and my feelings but they make no sense to me. They are just there, happening as the event of the telephone call unfolds.

'Rachel and I found your Mum in bed this afternoon in a coma. We called the doctor and he has said that he doesn't think that she will come out of it, and will probably only last until tomorrow morning.' Ian pauses.

'OK.'

'Damian, I think it is important that you get up here to the Coast to be with your Mum as soon as possible.'

'Yes, of course,' I say.

'I think it's important that you come now, Damian. I don't think you should put this off.'

'Sure …' My voice maintains its best semblance of being blasé.

'OK, that's good. I've had to inform some of the Army people about the situation in order to get you on the phone. I hope you don't mind me doing that?'

'No, of course not.'

'OK, well I think they are going to arrange for you to get a flight from Melbourne up to The Coast as soon as possible. So check with them, and we'll see you soon.'

'OK, thanks Ian. I guess I'll see you soon.'

We say goodbye and I hang up.

There wasn't too much time to deeply consider the contents of the phone call. The moment the receiver touched its base, the door to the office reopened and the woman admin officer entered with a driver in tow, a friend of mine called Lance Corporal Moore. She looked as though every maternal instinct or urge she had ever had was returning to overwhelm her at that very moment, and nervously shuffled around behind the driver. She explained that the Army had booked me an evening flight from Melbourne leaving in a couple of hours, so we would have to move quickly. Lance Corporal Moore would take me to my room so I could get some fresh clothes before leaving for the airport. And so it was that I spent a little over an hour in the company of Lance Corporal Moore's abundant nervous energy as he drove me at breakneck speed to Melbourne's Tullamarine Airport where I narrowly avoided missing the plane which would fly me to Maroochydore during those last hours of my mother's life.

***

I'd lived in the presence and absence of my mother, Angie, for eighteen years. This is my story yet it is also a story about us both. Our two lives were always entwined in a sometimes painful, sometimes beautiful, but always loving mesh of interdependence. She was aged 24 when she gave birth to me and I was her first and only child. Like so many others of her generation, Angie rebelled against the social expectations of her parents' era by never marrying. She willingly embarked on a voyage of single parenthood. If Angie once loved my father she never spoke of it to me. The story she told me about their separation was uninteresting, and having played absolutely no role in our lives, my father has remained an entirely insignificant figure in my life.

After her relationship with my father, Angie never took another partner. This, coupled with the fact that her connection with her parents and two sisters was always minimal, left the two of us alone to find our own way in the world. Our journey together, while undertaken in relative isolation, was not free from other influences and throughout our eighteen years together we endured the constant company of mental illness, specifically *anorexia nervosa*. As my only parent and guardian, Angie was hopelessly flawed; as a friend and companion she was unintentionally crippling, but as a source of inspiration and strength, my mother was a champion.

I was born in Mt Gambier, South Australia, but I know as much about Mt Gambier as I do about the North Pole, which is precious little. A few months after I was born, we left my father and Australia behind and moved to Christchurch in New Zealand, her birth country. We remained there for about four years but I really have no memory of that time either. I do have some rather amusing soft focus 1980s family portrait photos of a very small me playing in the snow, but they are quite generic and unrevealing.

My earliest memories begin in Auckland. I have a jumble of small but distinct memories of seemingly random events, as if I'm flipping through TV channels and never staying on any long enough to understand the context of what I'm seeing.

I remember being at day care aged three or four and intentionally wetting my pants so I could feel more like the other kids. I remember getting a bike for Christmas and being confused because Santa had used one of our bed sheets as wrapping, yet I also had a sense that I shouldn't ask why. I remember falling through the springs of a friend's trampoline and trying not to cry; spending hours jumping off a jetty into the ocean with some other neighbourhood kids; and, I remember stealing a packet of cake decoration silver balls from a corner store. Looking back, it all seems fairly normal.

So there I was, by about the age of four living with Angie in Auckland, a sprawling metropolis characterised by its blend of British colonial heritage and a strong Maori indigenous culture. We frequently moved houses and suburbs. In the three years we lived in Auckland, before moving back to Australia, I attended four different schools, which meant making new friends every six months. During those years, Angie always seemed to be at work, and as a child it wasn't always clear to me what she was doing or where she was working. She was simply not around very much. She was a cook by trade, a craft that is not uncommon among people suffering *anorexia nervosa*. It's a fact that later struck me as cruelly ironic. She worked weeknights, presumably in a restaurant, and then on weekends, if she wasn't catering for a function, she would be busy doing renovations or gardening, getting her house ready to sell again. I was frequently alone, filling in those hours between the end of school and the start of sleep as best as I could. If I was lucky, Angie would work a day shift and eventually arrive home to cook me dinner. But if not, then there was always some food left in the fridge and I soon learnt to get something for myself. I would stay back after class to help 'clean up' even when there was no cleaning to do; I tactically prolonged the walk home from kindergarten or school for as long as I could. I became adept at killing time. I made friends with anyone I could and would invite myself over for afternoon tea as regularly as I dared. For me, being at home alone was something to be avoided. An uninhabited house is a cold and lonely place for a single child. The various houses I lived in, empty of people, were nothing more than a collection of things, about as comforting and inviting as a furniture store. Each empty house was no home, just a towering collection of odd nick-knacks beyond my reach. I would find myself sitting in the middle of a very large room, just waiting for something to happen.

***

The memories I have of my mother actually being present during those early years almost always involve walking. Angie was a frantic walker. If she wasn't heaving a shovel in the backyard or chopping vegies in a kitchen, she had me pounding the pavements or the parks of Auckland at high velocity. Even when I was four. I didn't understand her behaviour: her unrelenting drive to do things and the absolute urgency with which she did everything. If walking meant charging along at full-steam-ahead then so be it. If weekends were for working twelve to fourteen hour days in the garden, I accepted it. And if parents never ate anything in front of their kids, then that was normal to me. It was later, once I reached adolescence, that I came to learn that her manic expense of energy – both in her working life and her private life – her aversion to eating and her distance from her family were all symptoms of her life-long battle with *anorexia*.

One of our regular haunts for these insane bouts of walking was one part of Cornwall Park, a huge public domain covering about one hundred hectares located in an inner suburb of Auckland. Its central point is a hill with a single large tree on its peak earning it the affectionate name, One-Tree Hill. A Maori name for the hill is Maungakiekie, after a vine found there. For a time, Angie worked at the park's kiosk and restaurant, cooking and serving lunches and afternoon teas as well as catering for the occasional function, for a wedding or for a business group. While she was working there, I attended school not far away in Remuera Road. It was a great bustling place filled with big children and big buildings surrounded by a six-foot high red brick wall. In a back corner of the school grounds there was a large fig tree. I, along with scores of other children, would delight in playing around the roots of the tree and searching its numerous hidey-holes for juicy treats. How to eat a fig is still a bit of a mystery, and as a child it seemed inconceivable to me to put one of those squishy, leathery brown lumps into my mouth. Each day after school I would cross the road beyond the red brick wall and walk the kilometre or two from the school gate up to the Cornwall Park kiosk where I would wait for Mum to finish work. Most of this twenty to thirty minute walk could be done on the soft grassy grounds of the park; it was simply a matter of climbing over the five-foot stone wall that encircled the park to immediately be transported from city to country life.

Large sections of the park's lower grounds had been leased to sheep farmers and a groundsman and his family still lived there in a stone cottage. There were scattered remnants of other colonial dwellings throughout the park. My favourite was a cobbled staircase that led up from the road to a building that no longer existed. After school I would wander alone along the inside edge of the great stone wall, talking to the sheep and kicking up great heaps of oak leaves from the old trees that also shadowed the wall around the park. Those afternoon walks home were always leisurely and filled with boyhood adventures inspired by modern legends such as 'Star Wars' and 'Indiana Jones'. On one particular afternoon I stumbled upon a still warm but dead pigeon as I made my way through the oak leaves, crawling on hands and knees, throwing my school bag ahead of me as if there was not enough room for the two of us in my imaginary World War II escape tunnel. I had never seen a dead animal before and was completely fascinated by it. I gave up my 'great escape' tunnel adventure and took to flying my inter-galactic space pigeon, complete with flapping wings, all the way through the park to its landing pad on the back steps of the kiosk. At five-thirty when Mum finished work, she came out to find me sitting on the back step as usual, except this time I had my slowly stiffening pigeon for company. Enchanted with my new friend, I had been eagerly awaiting Mum's arrival to show off my find. The bird was soft like my teddies yet functional like my plastic 'Star Wars' space ships, and best of all I had found it for free. I was devastated when I realised that Mum did not share my enthusiasm. The funeral was a brief affair with Mum tossing the bird into the dumpster and saying a few sharp words followed by a wake of vigorous hand washing in the kiosk toilets. She was a good mother – she taught me hygiene but not respect for the dead, at least as far pigeons were concerned.

After work, weather permitting, Mum and I would set off on one of her training sessions as if she was preparing for an Olympic speed walking event. We would do a single lap of the park, sticking to the main circle road that snaked its way up to the peak and back down to the kiosk. The park's flora varied little and mostly reflected both the open grazing lands of the rest of New Zealand and the oak-lined park-ways of 'Mother England'. Angie was, like so many others of her generation and ilk, an unwitting product of her British heritage, her observations of landscape and life rarely venturing beyond a simple comparative remark about life in Great Britain. In that sense Cornwall Park was a wonderland. There was a dedicated area of manicured garden bed where sections were sponsored by one community citizens' club or another. On the eastern side where the wind seemed to blow incessantly there was a rock pit where people had fun arranging the rocks to spell out variations of *I-Love-You*, and the like.

The route we would take included five cattle grid crossings which I loved to hop carefully across, and sometimes, if I was lucky, we would detour down to the kids' swing park in the distant southern corner where Mum would wait impatiently while I ran the gamut of swings, slides, planks, and poles.

Although there were many opportunities for short-cuts, it would have defeated Angie's goal of relentless walking to take a short-cut back to the car. One such area of the park that was intentionally avoided by my 'aspiring gold medallist' mother was a rather dark and ominous grove of pine trees in the very last section of the park before we went back up to the kiosk and the car. Each day we traced the outer edge of the pine grove as we neared the end of our walk, and each day my suspicion and apprehension about the place grew. I would be tired by the time we reached the grove, desperately trying to keep up half a dozen paces behind Mum.

I can remember one evening when I was still aged four, that it was almost dark by the time we reached the pines and I felt an eeriness creep over me. Their floor of spongy, matted fallen needles, their sticky sweet musk sap and their quiet arching limbs reaching up to close out the sky seemed an entirely other-worldly place.

Mum had been a bit late finishing work. Winter was on its way and the days were getting shorter. Dark rain clouds were beginning to gather on the horizon but we took off on our walk, regardless. In my imagination we passed an invisible house but did not stop to go up the stairs to knock on its invisible door. We bypassed the children's playground and marched on up toward the peak. A staggering wind blowing at its summit seemed to want to blow the great single tree onto its side. I could see from above that someone had written 'All Blacks' in the rock pit but didn't have time to think through the meaning of the words as we set off once again. As darkness fell we approached the pine grove. Without saying a word, Mum cut diagonally through the grove rather than going around the bottom of the hill and then back up. I blinked in disbelief as she suddenly turned off the road and marched straight into the black forest. For a moment I hesitated on its edge, afraid and confused, as I watched her figure disappear into a ghostly darkness.

I looked longingly back down the path that I had walked a hundred times before. I desperately wanted to just run its length, circling around the pine grove and then back up to the safety of the car. But I couldn't abandon my mother, I couldn't leave her in there alone. What if she turned back and couldn't find me? What if she became disoriented looking for me? What if I waited by the car and she never came out? I had no choice but to brave the darkness. With Mum now an almost indiscernible dot in the distance, I couldn't wait any longer. A great ball of fear grew in my stomach as I descended deeper into the grove, my steps slow and deliberate while the rest of the world closed off behind me. The grove couldn't have extended more than a couple of hundred metres in any one direction, yet to me it seemed that within minutes I was lost forever. I could no longer see Angie. My apprehension and paranoia had slowed me to a near crawl. I stopped still and spun around looking in every direction for a sign of her, the great pines towering above my head like the bars of an oversized cage.

I panicked. My imagination raced. I ran blindly in circles, crying and calling out to her, the fear that I had lost her forever mounting as I ran. I expected to find her crumpled body on the ground, motionless but still warm like the pigeon's corpse. When I think about it now I realise that I might have run around the grove taking the path of safety that I knew so well, but instead I chose to confront my own fear for the sake of my mother. It was in those moments as I ran through the woods that I first became aware of the fragility of her relationship with me. Over the years my frantic panic was replaced by a hopeless wondering until eventually I came to realise that she wouldn't ever be there to support me. It was up to me to find her, to help her, and to save us both.

Except for this one incident I'd assumed that my early childhood, though somewhat devoid of adult supervision, was for the most part quite normal. That understanding would change over time. I did eventually find my way out of the evil pine grove, and I found Angie waiting on the road up at the kiosk. She was not only safe and sound, but also somehow disinterested in my tale of woe. That night when we returned home I gave myself a shower while Mum prepared something for dinner. I came out in my flannelette pyjamas and sat alone at the dining table as I always did. Waiting for me was a glass of water and my plate of mashed potatoes, lightly steamed vegies and a fillet of unknown fish. Angie was nowhere to be seen.

My early childhood now seems such a long time ago and my memories have been reduced to flashes of only the most vivid events. But I know how I felt then. In spite of my panic over a sense of being lost in the woods that day, I know I feared more for Angie's safety than I did for my own. Even at that early age, I had a sense that her well-being was more at risk than my own, and that I would have to play a role in taking care of her. But I was still too young to understand that my situation was not normal, or that my relationship with my mother was not healthy. Despite this, there must have been others around me who did take notice, who did see a problem, and to some degree did take action. After having attended about three schools and lived in three houses over about a year and a half without things at home having improved, I was sent away to boarding school.

Chapter 2

The solution to my mother's mounting problems with concerned neighbours and social workers was to send me to boarding school when I was five years old. I actually had a say in which boarding school she sent me to, which seemed to me entirely wonderful. Mum and I took a weekend trip to a town called Hamilton, a couple of hours south of Auckland, where we looked at two different boarding schools. As we wandered around the grounds of each school on mini-tours led by the respective principals, my mind was not focused on evaluating the merits of the two institutions. Instead it was singularly directed to remember a lie. I was trying desperately hard to remember to tell anyone who asked that I was aged six and not five. The youngest age that either school admitted a child was seven, or turning seven in the first term; yet here I was only five and would only be turning six at the start of the school year. I was a year too young. Of the two schools we looked at, Southwell and Cumberline, it was Southwell, the more 'modern' of the two, which was my choice even though I was limited by what little I actually took in of the two schools.

I was too young to realise then, but on reflection it would seem that Angie must have been in a quite desperate situation to have been willing to send me away to boarding school. Mum had spent her entire schooling as a boarder despite the fact that her parents lived close to a school and also despite an option which would have allowed her to attend as a day girl. Her stories of school life were filled with her sense of rejection and loneliness. Later in life, when I thought back on Mum speaking about the misery of her childhood, I would wonder what role boarding school had played in her developing *anorexia*. But as a child the idea never occurred to me.

Whatever the odds against my mother years later trying to enrol her son in boarding school, she persisted and won. I played my part as a seven-year-old to perfection and fooled everyone. I was formally accepted into Southwell Preparatory School for Boys, so Mum and I made a second trip down to the school a weekend or two later to visit the uniform shop. We met 'Matron' who was the school nurse and the person who would take care of me when I arrived on the bus just a couple of weeks later. Next was a trip into town to buy me my first cricket bat, the one non-compulsory accessory that we were assured was still a necessity. I was convinced that this was going to mark my transition from childhood to manhood. The uniform, the cricket bat, the buildings – they all radiated an air of tradition in which I was soon to play a part, and for that reason I was delighted. Even as a child, I tried to refrain from being childishly excited, as I was desperate to show myself off as a proper young gentleman.

Back home on my sixth birthday, Mum threw a small party for me, the guest list made up mostly of her friends and their children who were consequently my friends. The event doubled as a farewell party, and without much in the way of encouragement I proudly modelled the various ensembles of my new school uniform for the pleasure of those present. The black and blue pin-striped woollen blazer, knee high socks and garters, the floppy summer golfer's cap sporting the school crest on its crown, a grey cotton shirt, and a blue striped tie, slacks for winter, sandals for summer – I looked so good in all of this attire I thought I could have passed for an eleven-year-old.

A few days later I stood next to Mum on the concrete floor of the bus transit centre, watching a man load my bag under the bus along with a hundred other identical Southwell bags.

'Mum, I don't want to go,' I said, holding her hand and looking up at her.

At first she didn't seem to hear me, as she continued to stare off into space while squeezing my hand.

'Mum ...' My voice was getting a bit shaky. 'I don't want ...'

I stopped mid-sentence as she dropped down onto her knees next to me and embraced me in an overwhelming hug. She held my head close to her body and softly wept. 'I know, baby ... I know ...'

***

Southwell was a school built on the memory of fine English traditions. Its stone Anglican chapel was hand built in the 1930s by boys who were boarding there at the time and the playing fields were as green and lush as those that patchwork the rolling hills of England. The grandeur and mystique of the school grounds inspired a sense of wonder and fear. So foreign was my environment that Mum now seemed a world away. As a 'junior' I was mixed in with eleven other First and Second Form boarders under the watchful eye of 'Matron'. To my child's eye she seemed perhaps in her fifties, a spinster who transported her rotund body around the school grounds in a crisp starched white nurse's uniform. Her behaviour and appearance were predictably stereotypical. Her medical bedside manner was efficient and curt, while her authoritarian role over us younger kids was a perfect mix of brisk, clear, no-

nonsense boundaries and melting maternal compassion. Matron was probably the polar opposite of my mother. But for the hundred or so boys who lived at the school, she was all we had and we loved her dearly.

During the day the school ran much like any other. There would be an influx of dayboys not long after eight o'clock in the morning, teachers who did not live on school grounds would arrive, and a normal day of lessons would follow. Come sundown things would change. The school took on a ghostly ambience, where the boarders would rattle around the vacant and unlit buildings, like predatory animals momentarily freed from their zoo enclosures.

The elation felt by most kids as they ride their bikes freely around the neighbourhood after school was not permitted for us. Instead, our free time between the end of classes and dinner was nearly always taken within the enclosed stone walls of one inner quadrangle or another. Looking back, I now see it as suspiciously like exercise time in a maximum security prison. Twelve junior boys were separated into our own dorm room downstairs, adjacent to the infirmary and Matron's residence. There, close to Matron, we were safer from night time loneliness and, more importantly, from the mischievous and cruel taunts of the older boys and the even crueller despotic punishments dealt out by the prefects.

After dinner there was time set aside for supervised homework, a compulsory evil that for me usually consisted of writing out my day's spelling mistakes one hundred times each. Following homework, we junior boys went back to Matron who supervised our showering and ablutions, then saw us into bed. On rare occasions, if Matron could find an appropriately educational and decidedly English Attenborough documentary on her television, she would invite us in to cram together like anchovies on her living room floor to watch it before going to bed. Generally though, our bedtime was an hour earlier than that of the older boys who were required to stay behind to do extra homework. Other than those odd times of watching television, we twelve younger boys would spend that precious hour of unsupervised 'sleep' time to push the boundaries of our dictatorial world. A popular game was for someone (often a blond haired Australian boy named Carter who was particularly unthreatened by the cane) to sneak out of the building and make his way to some distant location on the school grounds and leave something there. He would then return and dare another boy to retrieve the item after 'lights out' while attempting to avoid capture by the unspoken enemy, comprising other dorm masters and the older boys, as well as our beloved Matron.

Our first form classrooms were located on the far side of the school grounds, a perfect area of operation for Carter and his high-jinks. As soon as Matron had seen us all neatly tucked into bed and turned the lights out, Carter would be up and out the door. It would feel as if he'd been gone for an eternity, until finally I would hear the slow creak of the door hinge heralding his return.

'My tie is hanging on the third coat hook from the left, outside Mrs Graham's first form room ... who's going to go and get it?' was the kind of dare Carter would offer us. He would whisper excitedly as he skipped softly around the room, shaking people by the foot. I hardly ever went because I was always too scared of getting caught and caned. Someone else would invariably go. Rowe, Baird, Jones, there was usually one boy ready to take up Carter's challenge.

I lived in mortal fear of the cane. I had witnessed it being administered to boys often enough to know what it was like. It repulsed a sense of humanity in me not just to know that it happened but also to have to watch as grown men would repeatedly flog a boy until he collapsed, crying, unable to stand. The humiliation carried as much weight as the physical abuse and the dorm master seemed to relish in both. The thought of it still sickens me and I struggle to think how my mother could have allowed the possibility that I might suffer it when she couldn't have been so naive as not to know it was happening to other boys.

Thanks to Carter I heard the swish and cry of boys being caned all too often. When one of our number was caught 'out-and-about' during sleep time he would be dragged back to our little dorm room. The door would be flung open, lights thrown on, and the dorm master would demand everyone out of bed for a caning in his office. In these moments I would deliver an Oscar award-winning performance of feigning sleep. I figured I was doing a good enough job keeping everyone fooled into thinking that I was seven and not six so I could surely convince them that I was asleep. And I was convincing. When all the other boys had filed out of the room and the master was still at the door spitting out, 'Cooper, Cooper, get up boy … Didn't you hear me? I said get out of bed!' I would remain stubborn, unmoving, and ultimately with an unblemished bottom.

Then one night as it was getting late it all came to a horrible end. Carter had already been up to his old tricks a few times: a hat on the door handle of the gymnasium, a shoe on the tennis court, and a belt on the back step of the kitchen. Normally he would have called it a night once the older boys had finished their homework and were returning to the dorm. But Carter, eager to push things that bit further, announced to the group that he would be going out again and this time it would be a special trip. Excited, seduced by the danger, we waited for his return. I got up to stare out of the window into darkness, looking for any sign of his reappearance. Carter, brazen as ever, returned by throwing open the door in mock dorm-master style, creating general fright in scaring us all, and then causing great cheers of laughter. He didn't turn the light on though. He was daring, but not stupid. He jumped up onto his bed and in a voice that was barely a whisper, demanded a volunteer. 'Which one of you chickens has the guts to go this time?' he taunted. 'I'm not saying where it is until someone agrees to go. So who's it going to be?'

As exciting as it was, no one jumped at the opportunity. The more daring boys of the group had already been out earlier in the night, so the prospect of going out again so close to the end of homework time for the older boys, was not good.

'Come on … one of you sissies must have the guts to do it!' Carter went on.

'I will do this.' Jebin, a roundish Indian boy with a soft voice, responded from out of the corner of the room.

'Great! Great! Great!' Thrilled, Carter jumped up and down on his bed and clapped his hands. 'You're perfect for this one, Heebie-Jeebie!'

Wearing his cotton summer pyjamas, Jebin got up out of bed and walked over to stand in the middle of the room to face Carter.

'Right, Heebie-Jeebie.' Carter stopped jumping around and became serious. 'One of my sports shoes is balancing on top of the beam that holds our tyre swing rope above the fort outside our classrooms.'

The fort was a two storey wooden structure that wouldn't pass an Occupational Health and Safety test administered by a drunkard. The tyre swing was suspended by a rope attached to a thick wooden beam that extended out from the roof of the fort. The rope dropped down two storeys from the beam, suspending the tyre about a foot off the ground. A wicked grin on Carters' face began to make sense to us all as we tried to imagine poor Jebin negotiating his way out onto the beam, to the shoe, and then down the rope.

Seeming unperturbed, Heebie-Jeebie set off, sneaking out the door, down the hallway and then outside. We watched him from behind the safety of our bedroom windows until he disappeared into the night. Then we waited in steely silence for our champion's return. We waited longer than we ought to have. It didn't occur to me at the time, but the older boys should have returned from homework over the time we waited and they hadn't returned. When we heard a siren somewhere off in the distance, no one said anything. Excitement turned to nervous tension as each boy soberly returned to his bed to lie quietly and wait. The night dragged on. Eventually we heard scattered movement outside, people coming and going. Then someone went into Matron's quarters, but no one came to us. The older boys came back, went about their ablutions and quietly went to bed. The silence, coupled with Jebin's ongoing absence, was more terrifying than any enraged dorm master could ever possibly be. Jebin was never seen again. We were informed by Matron the next day that he'd had an accident and had gone to hospital. Nothing more ever said about the incident and while no one was ever caned, Carter put his adventures on hold.

***

Although I'd managed to avoid a caning by pretending to be asleep during those after-hours antics, I knew I was not always going to be so lucky. A few months after the Jebin accident, I received word to report immediately to the headmaster, a man who generally had nothing to do with the boys unless it involved some kind of disciplinary action. My mind raced with thoughts of what possible reprehensible activities I had committed. I remembered that I had been playing ball against the wall of the dining hall with a Third Form boy the day before. A cook had come out and told us in no uncertain terms to go away. That had to be it. So my time had come and they had finally caught me, I thought ... the cook had taken it up with the headmaster and now he was going to flog me for it ... I would just have to take it like a man. I trembled my way up to his office, reached the door and took a last deep breath before knocking.

'Come in,' called the aged-malt voice from inside.

I entered the room, closing the door behind me. The interior of the head's office had the same sense of grandeur as the rest of the school. Its focal point was a great oak desk in the middle of the room, its top lined with deep green leather, its masterfully turned legs reaching down to detailed feet. Two matching green leather Chesterfield arm chairs faced the desk. Scattered across the walls were old photos of previous headmasters and portraits of prominent people, including the Queen. The headmaster, a tall thin man probably in his mid-sixties, with drawn cheeks and deep-set eyes, sat patiently in his high-backed chair on the other side of the desk. Rarely seen without a pipe in his mouth, he seemed to blend perfectly with the ambience of the room, as if he himself had come from an antique dealer's shop.

'Good afternoon, Mr Cooper. Thank you for coming in to see me.'

His melodic, grandfatherly voice did nothing to calm my nerves. My stare was fixed on his cane, which was leaning against the wall behind him.

'I have called you here today because I would like to discuss some matters concerning your mother.' He spoke to me as if I were a business associate, a fellow gentleman, and reflecting now, I wouldn't have been surprised if he had offered me a brandy.

The previously inevitable advancement of the old railway clock's second hand seemed to pause in time at the mention of my mother. A seed of hope took root in the pit of my stomach and a wave of relief washed over me as my fear momentarily subsided. So gripped was I by the fear of the cane, so perfectly had the school fostered an environment of pain and retribution based on the ethos of 'spare the rod and spoil the child', that the only response I could manage at the mention of my mother was profound relief. My world had been so reduced to the immediate, that Angie was no longer important to me. I imagine now that if I'd been called up because she was dying, to my young self that still would have been a fate preferable to caning.

'Your mother contacted me earlier this week to inform me of some changes to her living arrangements and to discuss the option of you staying on here at Southwell,' he continued. 'Perhaps you might like to take a seat for a moment.'

'Yes, sir,' I found the courage to reply.

'Damian ...' I was surprised that he actually knew my first name and was even more surprised that he was using it.

'Your mother has advised me that as of yesterday morning she no longer resides here in New Zealand and she does not plan to return.' He paused, perhaps for effect or perhaps for me to gain some clearer understanding of what he had just said.

'I understand this could be something of a shock to you, son, but rest assured that it will not affect your time here at Southwell. After some discussion, your mother has agreed that you will stay on here with us, at least until the end of the year.'

He continued speaking, describing some of the finer details of what would be happening to me during the several school holidays to come.

'I shall have Mr Overton make some enquiries over the following weeks in regard to finding you some place to stay. Clearly, you will not be able to stay on school grounds during the break and as your mother has left no indication as to where she would like you to be, I think it only appropriate that we find you some other family to go to. Though this is somewhat unorthodox, we here at Southwell pride ourselves on ...'

He went on to talk about some other administrative matters, but I had tuned out. I retreated into my own mind, to a place where, moments before, my only concern had been the cane. Now, that fear had been entirely replaced by a sense of emptiness. A void. My head spun at how quickly the world I lived in had come crashing down. Even at Southwell, which seemed so far away from her, so protected, a place made stable and secure by its stone walls and its draconian rules, her presence, or lack of it, could still cripple me. I wanted to break down and cry. I wanted someone else to be responsible for her, and to tell me it was okay to live my life and not have to worry about her. Deep inside, I knew that there was no one else to look after her. Even here at boarding school, I felt she needed me. Her *anorexia* had made victims of us both.

That day marked the second time in my life that I had become acutely aware of the growing loneliness that was walking in my shadow. A loneliness born out of a total absence of trust in my mother. Unlike the time I lost her in the pine grove, this time I had nowhere to run to. There was no 'edge of the forest' to be reached in this nightmare. I was completely alone. Abandoned. Left in the omnipotent care of a stranger and his caning rod. I didn't cry. I just let him finish what he wanted to say and left. I spent the rest of the afternoon alone, wandering around the school grounds aimlessly while I tried to remember her. What she looked like and how she acted. I tried to picture her smiling, and to remember the warmth of her embrace. I wanted to be able to smile too and to feel good about her. But mostly I tried to imagine what my life would be like if I never saw her again. Later that night I lay in bed with the moonlight spilling through the uncurtained window above my bed and pictured Roald Dahl's B.F.G. or 'Big Friendly Giant' reaching through the window and carrying me away forever.

I managed to finish my year at Southwell without incident and without another visit to the headmaster's office. I spent school holidays and long weekends with the families of whichever boy the head managed to arrange. The dorm master would give me whatever instructions were needed.

I saw first-hand how other kids lived with their parents. I played cricket in the summer and rugby in the winter and despite everything, I left the Southwell school with mostly fond memories. Looking back, I now feel as if I've lived the boyhood adventures of a modern Dickensian character. At the time, I know I was very unhappy. Every day that I was there I felt as if I was taking a step closer to the unknown. Yes, one step closer to the end of the year when I would be pushed out the front gate and back into my mother's life. I had realised early on in the year that I did not feel good about returning to her and that although she loved me, Mum was capable of making me very unhappy.

My year at Southwell marked a significant and, sadly, a premature turning point in my life. At age six there'd been a change in my awareness brought about by a combination of isolating factors. The reversal in thinking that I undertook that year could not have been more clearly pronounced. I gained a new perspective on myself. Prior to going to Southwell, my life had seemed to me to be relatively normal, but from that point onwards I lost all illusions about what little childhood dependence I could enjoy. I began to learn the relative nature of trust as I became increasingly aware of the physical and mental symptoms of my mother's illness.

Chapter 3

On the last day of the year at Southwell, amid the fanfare and excitement of finishing school, I joined about half of the students and took a chartered bus full of chocolates and laughter back up to Auckland. While most of the boys were collected by their families at the bus interchange when we arrived, I, having no family to meet me, waited on the other side of the huge building for another bus to take me to the international airport. It had all been prearranged. The bus people knew to expect me, the flight ticket had been booked and the airline staff finally nestled me safely into the first-class waiting lounge as soon as I checked in. It was during those in-between times, the people-less parts of getting from one check-in counter to another, that I began to feel grown up.

The contrast between my school life of rigid and constant supervision and walking unescorted, freely, through a major international airport was intoxicating. I was alone but it was different from feeling alone at boarding school. I felt free in the world and that was tremendously exhilarating. I savoured that feeling from the moment I boarded the aircraft on my first solo international flight, Auckland to Brisbane. Although the transit in Sydney was entirely uneventful, I basked in the magnitude of the experience. With the exception of watching the in-flight film *Cocoon* by Ron Howard, I spent most of my three-and-a-half hour journey wondering what to expect of my new home in Queensland.

All my imaginings were fuelled by the one source of information on Queensland that I had been able to obtain. This was a faded souvenir tea towel displaying poorly printed images of the Great Barrier Reef, the Big Pineapple, Fraser Island and other assorted attractions, interspersed with an occasional coffee stain. However, on arrival my tea towel fantasies seemed to evaporate in a muggy Queensland summer haze. It was not the landscape that differed from my imagination so much ... not the stifling humidity, the look of the people, nor the accent with its corresponding lackadaisical style in the use of the English language, similar to the English of New Zealand yet different. Rather, it was my mother that struck a stark contrast to the images in my memory. She was no longer the beautiful woman I remembered. So profound was the difference, so horrifying the apparition that greeted me, that all the excitement and anticipation I had enjoyed on the plane immediately disappeared.

At the time, Brisbane international airport was little more than an oversized demountable building, which only intensified the thick Queensland humidity. I could see the snaking heat rising off the tarmac, and the smell of aviation fuel was still in my nose as I made my way through the customs area of the airport. As I rounded the corner into the public arrivals lounge, a bobbing sea of unfamiliar faces confronted me. I stared at the faces before me, watching as individuals randomly sprang forward from the mob to embrace loved ones from among the rest of the passengers behind me. For a moment I was struck with a fear that I had been on the wrong plane or that no one would be there to meet me. My fears were not so much allayed, but redirected when I finally spotted Angie tentatively emerge from the crowd. My hands tightened around the handle of my trolley bag as I developed a sickening feeling, first of sadness and then embarrassment, as the skeletal form that was now my mother moved slowly toward me.

Angie was dangerously emaciated. Her hair, although dyed auburn red, was brittle and straw like. The twinkle of delight that would normally shine in her crystal green eyes on seeing me was lost in the dark, sunken recesses of her face. The dimensions of her skull were striking; her cheek bones were ledges above the gaping depressions of her face; her jaw seemed suspended like a science classroom model skeleton. Her gums, which were a patchy dark purple, had receded, exposing her teeth above the enamel and causing them to decay. Her skin was paper-thin and covered in abrasions from minor accidents. A thick pasty sort of smell hung in the air, which I found out later was cod liver oil. A thin coat of oil lathered her skin, its rank smell intensified by the humidity, making it inescapable. Her skin hung loosely on her frame, revealing the contours of her bones where normally flesh would hide the inner workings of the body. She hugged me in an insubstantial embrace. I held her as tightly as I dared and imagined that I was holding the body of a dying alien, prematurely hatched from its cocoon, which I had just seen on the flight movie.

Nothing was said as we made our way from the airport terminal to the car under a blistering sun. The awkwardness was palpable. I sat in the passenger seat with my knees closed together and pulled up against my chest while I stared out of the window, trying to understand who this thing was that sat next to me.

'Did you have a good flight?' Her question cut into my thoughts as a far off reminder of something very familiar.

'Yes, thank you,' I dutifully replied.

'Well, that's good. It was right on time which is always nice.' She was making an effort, her soft clear voice catching my attention.

'And there's not a cloud in the sky today, which is what it's like here most of the time, not like back in old N.Z.'

She spoke with what seemed like a sense of growing hope in her voice.

'Mind you, you're probably going to feel the heat for the first little while. It gets hot enough to fry an egg on the bonnet here, but the beach isn't far away.'

Slowly, as I listened, I began to realise that buried somewhere beneath that hellish façade was the soft kind mother of my memories, and with every word her voice – which was unchanged – drew me back in.

'I have gotten us a lovely little place right by the beach, which you're just going to love. And, sweetie, I think we are really going to be able to stay here together this time.'

'Okay,' I said.

I spent my seventh birthday playing in the sand at a beach on the Sunshine Coast. True to her word Mum, was renting a small fibro home flat close to the ocean while she looked around for somewhere better to buy. Having already been there for close to a year she'd made some friends through a small church group that she had become involved with, and she was particularly friendly with another single mother, Leanne, who lived a few streets away.

Leanne was an attractive young woman with dark hair and big, dairy cow, brown eyes. She had two children, both a few years younger than me. I liked Leanne and she liked me, always giving me a huge welcoming smile whenever I saw her. If I wasn't at Leanne's playing with her kids, I was riding my bike around to explore my new world, a world that felt a million miles away from the cold stone walls of Southwell. I learnt to boogie board and fumbled around with surfboards whenever I could get someone to lend me one. I knew all the short cuts through backyards to the beach, and which take-away shops had the best video game machines. I was stupidly happy – but Mum was not.

One night while we were still in our little white-washed beach flat watching television, Mum told me that she was going to bed because she was tired and that I shouldn't bother waking her in the morning as she intended to sleep in. She was normally up with the sunrise and out the door to walk along the beach before it became crowded. I wondered about it for a few moments then slipped back into watching television. The night wore on and I put myself to bed without thinking any more about it. In the morning I diligently obeyed her command and did not attempt to wake her while I made myself some breakfast. Then I rode my bike for hours to pass the time. It must have been mid-morning when I returned and found her still in bed.

I decided to wake her. By that time in the morning the closed bedroom had become stuffy and humid and the curtains were still drawn. I crept into the dark private chamber. She lay motionless on the bed, still covered by her doona.

'Mum?' I whispered into the darkness. 'Mum, it's nearly lunch time …' She made no indication of having heard me.

'Mum?' I said again, this time a bit louder. 'Mum, it's time to get up.'

I reached down to touch her gently on the shoulder. She felt cold. I had had no experience with death. I didn't know the signs to look for, but at that moment I instinctively knew something was wrong.

'Mum!' I called with a panicked edge in my voice, no longer whispering at all.

'Mum, Mum, you have to get up … please, Mum.'

I started to shake her by the shoulder, but her head just seemed to loll on the pillow as if she wasn't there. I called to her but she was far, far away, down the other end of the beach on a windy day.

Something was terribly wrong. I checked and saw that she was still breathing though only ever so lightly so I ran out of our front door and down the walkway to our neighbour's flat. I pounded on the door with my fists, screaming for the neighbours to come out and help me. When the old man finally came to the door, tears were streaming down my face as I blurted out what I could.

Back at our place, I dragged him down the hall into our flat and then into Mum's room. He looked shocked as he made some futile attempts to wake her, then quickly retreated to our telephone to call an ambulance.

Fear wrapped its fingers so firmly around my heart that I thought it might stop beating. I couldn't stand around and wait, so I ran. I ran as fast as I could, my bare feet skipping over prickly grass and rough gravel without slowing as I worked my way through the houses and back streets until I reached Leanne's place. I was out of breath and sweating from running flat out in the 35 degree summer heat, my tear-soaked cheeks burned red and my swollen feet very sore.

Immediately, Leanne grabbed me and her two kids and pushed us all into her Kingswood station wagon. She drove as fast as the old car could carry us, back to where Mum lay unconscious. We arrived in time to see ambulance officers wheeling her out of our house, strapped to a bed with an oxygen mask over her face. The old man who had called the ambulance stood with his wife in the doorway of their flat. I watched from the back seat of Leanne's car as she ran out to talk to the ambulance men. Her kids hugged each other, while I hugged myself and whimpered. The doors closed on my mother and the ambulance left. Leanne locked up our flat, and took us back to her house where she made some lunch and tried to explain as best she could what had happened. My mum had heavily overdosed and might not live.

I stayed with Leanne for a while, visiting Mum each day at the hospital, but mostly just playing with her kids in the sand pit in their backyard. I wasn't allowed to go off riding and adventuring as I normally did, and while it was comforting to be with Leanne, I missed my freedom.

I was relieved when Mum eventually returned home. My freedom reinstated, I was able to resort to my former independence. That first suicide attempt, in the small beach flat in Maroochydore, marked the start of what I have to come to think of as the darkest days of my childhood. Undoubtedly, my mother's illness had a profound and lasting effect on a range of people – particularly members of her family who felt so cut off and helpless. But I'm sure it affected no one more profoundly than myself. Over the following nine or ten years I lived in constant fear that I would again find my mother in a similar situation, a fear that was repeatedly validated, and only diminished through my psychological and emotional isolation from her.

Not long after the suicide attempt, Mum bought a two-bedroom apartment on the top floor of an apartment complex in Alexandra Headland. With a swimming pool, tennis court, ping pong table room, a balcony with views of the beach, and proximity to a school camp bushland reserve. My new home was a delight.

Mum had been given an early share of her parents' eventual inheritance not long after I'd been born. When she'd left my father, she'd had nowhere to live. Her parents gave her enough money to buy a small flat in Christchurch. From that humble beginning, through a series of sales and purchases she accrued enough money to buy a place by the beach. Mum owned that Alexandra Headland apartment for five years, the longest period she ever lived anywhere. I only spent about two and a half of those years actually living in the apartment with Mum. I spent the rest of the time living with an assortment of families and friends while Mum went in and out of hospital.

Sometimes she would go willingly to a general admissions ward. Other times she was committed to psychiatric wards, or she would just go there directly. When I was not at home with her, I lived with a series of different people – and depending on the circumstances and time permitted, I was generally able to choose who I stayed with.

My real family, Mum's parents and her two sisters, still lived in New Zealand. When possible, Mum would arrange for me to fly over by myself to spend summer holidays and Christmas breaks with her mother and father, Bette and Jack, or with one of her two sisters, Jo or Chris. That was often more about giving the families I had been living with throughout the year a rest than reflecting Mum's close ties with her immediate family. Whether it was with our real family, a distant relative, a friend from school, or a sympathetic teacher, I always seemed to have somewhere to stay. Social services were never involved, which I guess was largely due to Mum's involvement with the church. There always seemed to be enough good people around who were willing to take me in. No one ever felt that there was any need to report anything to government authorities.

Chapter 4

It wasn't long after we'd moved into the Alexandra Headland apartment at the end of the summer holidays that I enrolled in Mooloolaba State Primary School. We didn't know anyone in the area and Mum was still dangerously unwell. Following her first suicide attempt she had been constantly monitored by health services, and being so unwell at that particular time, she agreed to go into hospital voluntarily. This was a concession that she very rarely made. She would normally avoid hospital at all costs, but on the upside it afforded her the opportunity to be involved in finding me an alternative place to stay.

Given the choice, I would have gladly opted for an old-fashioned suicide attempt, ambulance ride, and play-it-by-ear technique, than knowingly go through with the debacle that eventually ensued. Sounds tough, I know, but this whole episode was tough on me, too. I remember starting school at Alexandra Headland in my not-quite-the-official school colour Bonds t-shirt, carrying a little more than the prescribed quota of puppy fat for my age and brandishing a slightly lofty New Zealand accent. I felt decidedly out of place. That feeling was magnified tenfold one particular day when a special all-school assembly was called. Everyone assembled under the cover of the ball courts. I had no idea what to expect. I was new to the school and new to the country, so there were many things that were a mystery to me compared with schooling in New Zealand. For instance, the staff at Mooloolaba State School were not quite sure what grade to put me in, so I ended up in a class with kids who were all older, and bigger, than me. As my class snaked its way in double file down toward the ball courts, having a cursive writing lesson interrupted to do so, I tried to act as casually as I could. Our class trailed into the back end of the ball court to be confronted by a seething mass of small restless bodies. I gingerly stumbled my way through the crowd, cautiously finding my footing in the midst of a sea of arms and legs. I found my spot and sat down cross-legged on the cold concrete floor of the ball courts, jostling with my classmates to get comfortable. We were jammed together, the closeness generating a kind of electric energy that kept everyone in high spirits. From where I sat I could make out the few classmates I had, and I sat smiling awkwardly.

The school principal stood on a small platform at the front of the crowd. It took a couple of bellows of 'Good Morning!' and some hushing from the teachers in the rear to bring the schoolkids into line.

'Good morning again, young people.' Mr Chatswood launched into his speech, using the opportunity of a special assembly to make a few extra announcements. My bottom was getting sore from sitting on the cold concrete. I glanced around at the other kids and was thinking about how different life was here in Queensland compared with boarding school in New Zealand. Mr Chatswood kept talking but I wasn't listening. I was thinking about Southwell with its insistence on ostentatious uniforms, its strict code of conduct and its commitment to corporal punishment. Mooloolaba State School couldn't have been more different. There was no real uniform, discipline seemed to be permanently on the brink of collapse, and if there was a punishment system I saw no evidence of it. But was I any happier here?

Eventually snatches of what the principal was saying filtered into my mind: 'This boy's Mum ... being new to this area ... a call for help ... parents will be asked ...'

Was he talking about me? I clutched my crossed legs to my chest with folded arms, burying my head into my knees. I peeped sideways at the other kids and felt my cheeks flush with shame. The more I listened, the more I was sure that he was talking about me.

'So if you think that your family might be able to offer some assistance to this boy and his mother, come and see me in my office after this assembly, or speak to one of your teachers.'

Why was he saying this about me? What sort of nightmare was this? Although he had not said my name, I felt sure that every child in the school knew that it was me he was talking about and they also knew the horrible person that my mother was. Without my knowledge, Mum had contacted the school. She had explained that she was going into hospital for three months and had asked if the school could help her find someone to take care of me. The principal had very kindly obliged.

To this day I can't think of another experience that has left me feeling more humiliated or more alone than I felt that morning. Every child at the school was instructed to go home and ask his or her parents if they would be willing to have that kid come and stay. That kid with the sick Mum, that kid with no family, that kid that's not really from around here. But fortune was smiling on me because it was a family that ran a holiday camp that eventually came to my rescue, and their two boys, who went to my school, Rick and David, would become two of the best friends I've ever had.

***

51

The older I became the greater my awareness of Mum's condition grew. I remember dreading having to live with her. I was more than ready to trade my freedom and independence for security and peace of mind. When kind-hearted familles would gleefully tell me that Mum was going to be coming home from hospital on the weekend, I would find it hard to share in their happiness. At least when she was in hospital I was safe in the knowledge that my home life would be stable, even if I were only a visitor in that home. Where ever I happened to be living at any given time – either at home with Mum, or somewhere else with a normal family – would dictate my prevailing mood. While I was living with Mum, generally the school bus would drop me off at the home of my friends, Rick and David, on the main road that ran parallel to the beach, about three hundred metres down the road from my place. The church camp grounds that their parents were in charge of covered about forty hectares of bushland that extended back from the beach towards Mum's apartment.

We three boys were the best of friends. Rick, who was my age, was a slight boy who generally preferred the company of a good book, while David was a few years older than me and loved surfing. David was both my hero and my best friend. Whenever possible, I would arrange things so that I could stay with their families while Mum was away. When I was not staying with them I would be forced, following a quick detour to the camp's cafeteria for afternoon tea, to take the slow and lonely walk up the road to my place. I tried to get in and out of there as quickly as possible. I only needed enough time to say hello, change out of my school clothes and into my board shorts, grab my boogie board and be out the door to meet David for an afternoon surf. This was always the most fearful part of my day, the moment when I would push the key into the front door lock, turn the handle and step inside, imagining what horrors might lie within.

The back external staircase of the apartment block had a rundown facade of moulding beige concrete-render and folded metal handrails. At the top they met a short brick-and-render passageway to door 14, Mum's door. As I stood there one afternoon, nothing of the goings-on inside were revealed to me as I stood outside. There I was, just the same as on every other afternoon, at the top of the stairs looking down the passage to the door and breathing deeply. It had been raining earlier in the day, a tropical downpour common at that time of year. There was now a puddle between me and the door. I waded through it without caring, my mind focused on what lay ahead. There was nothing to suggest that anything might be wrong inside, yet for some reason I felt more anxious than usual. I unlocked the rain-swollen door and shoved it open with my shoulder.

'Hello?' I called into the apartment. I dumped my bag in my room which adjoined the doorway. There was no answer.

'Mum, I'm home!' I called again, nudging the door shut with my bottom while I took off my shoes. I peered down the hall into the lounge and could see nothing.

'Mum?' I could hear the tension in my own voice now. Just the fact that she hadn't answered the first time I'd called out was enough to turn my stomach over from dread. I edged down the hall, torn between wanting and not wanting to know what would be around the corner.

From the lounge I could see almost all the rest of the house. There was no sign of Mum. I experienced a moment of relief in thinking she might just be out for a walk or down at the beach for a swim. Then I spotted a note on the kitchen bench and confidently walked over to read it. It was a large piece of paper folded in half. I opened it out and froze. Everything went silent except for the coursing blood being pumped into my head by my thundering heart. I felt physically sick. My hands were shaking and tears were forming in the corner of my eyes.

'No ... no, no, no, no!' I pleaded, feeling horribly betrayed, as I struggled to read Mum's hand-written last will and testament.

54

Still clutching the note, I looked around the room again, and this time I knew the signs to look for. I was not surprised to find them.

'Mum … ' I sobbed, as I followed the signs towards her bedroom. My body shaking, I looked inside. There she lay on her bed. I turned away and stood there with my back to her room, trembling, wishing I wasn't there.

I wanted desperately for someone to hold me and to tell me that everything was all right. I wanted to know why this was happening again and most of all I wished I could ensure that I would never have to face this moment again. But I was alone. I phoned the emergency 000 number and asked for the ambulance service. If I had known the direct number for the local station I wouldn't have bothered with the emergency switch because in my mind the damage was done and there was no need for anyone to rush. I went to my room and sat there in the silence of the small apartment. My subsiding sobs were all that I could hear now. I looked around my bedroom at my toys and clothes and I wondered how long it would be before I would sleep there again. I began to pack some things. My fear was slowly being replaced with hopeless anger as I kicked things around my room, trying to decide what was most important to take with me. I was filling in time. Distracting myself from the horror of thinking about my mother.

When I had finished packing I went to wait on the back steps for the ambulance. I couldn't stand to be inside any longer. When the ambulance officers arrived, I calmed down. I watched them park their van and clamber out with their equipment. I remained seated off to one side of the rough-textured concrete stairs with my overflowing school backpack at my feet in front of me. They came up the stairs without their stretcher bed and although I might have told them they would need it, I didn't. I had become indifferent. I had been through this sort of drama before.

They took their time making one more than extra trip up and down the flight of stairs before they finally took up the trolley. I just sat by and watched. I didn't say anything and neither did they. By the time they'd brought my mother down, I'd travelled the full gamut of emotions and was left drained and desensitised. I didn't want to feel things any more, and as they closed up the back of the ambulance, I believed I'd perfected the art of detachment. Dead or alive, it made no difference to me. I was numbed by the horror of seeing her like that. When they were ready to go I asked which hospital they were taking her to, assured them that I had neighbours to stay with, and then with my belongings on my back, I wandered down to Rick and David's parents' house with only a feeling of shame for having to once again impose on them.

These were the hardest experiences of my life and for a time they came one after another thick and fast. There were times when I wished she would be dead so it would be over, so I would no longer have to go on living in fear. It wasn't something I could turn off or escape. I was living with that intense fear every day. That moment of total powerlessness as the door to the apartment was pushed open, that moment of complete isolation from any kind of support.

One time I was taken to see her during one of her prolonged stays in hospital and found that she had been moved from her normal bed. The people I was living with at the time had driven me up to see my mother and then tactfully disappeared when I was about to go in to see her. So I approached a nurse. She told me that Angie had made an attempt on her own life during the night and was now being held in the suicide watch room located behind the nurse's counter. The nurse took me behind the counter and I was able to peer into the room through a glass peep hole reinforced with wire. I saw Angie tied to the bed, her hands and legs bound with thick padded leather straps, as she stared blankly at a wall. It was more than I could bear.

The nurse let me in and locked the door behind me. Angie turned her head and managed a tired smile but I didn't smile back – and I didn't approach her. I was tired too.

'Mum ...' I paused, trying to find the courage for what I was about to say. 'I can't ... I can't do this anymore. Do you understand?'

She made no response. She just kept looking at me through those empty eyes.

'I mean, you can't keep doing this to me. I don't want to have to keep being here when you wake up ... when you don't get it right. Do you understand? Do you see what I'm saying? I love you, Mum, but I just can't.'

If she had reached out to me, if she had been able to raise her arms, perhaps I would have crumpled – fallen to pieces emotionally, broken down. I would have run over into her embrace, feeling engulfed by her love. But she couldn't do anything.

'Mum, I want you make sure you get it right next time ... or never do it again. I just don't want be here ever again.'

Then I turned my back, knocked on the door for the staff to open it, and left.

I loathed seeing her in hospital, at first in the psych ward strapped to her bed and later in the general hospital being artificially sustained by an intravenous drip. It all seemed pointless. Yet despite everything, despite the fear and frustration, the loneliness and confusion, I loved her with all my heart. Angie was my mother and for that part of her I had all the love in the world. But she was also the victim of a horrible illness and for that I pitied her. And myself, which is why I spoke so harshly during those extreme times, I guess. I never resented her, only the illness. Not once did I feel let down or betrayed by her, I always saw it as the disease's doing.

Somehow I could always understand enough to separate the effects of the illness from the mother that loved me. In the same way that her love for me kept her alive, my love for her kept me functioning and happy.

Chapter 5

Even in the midst of her extreme illness and heartache, Angie would somehow find the energy to take us on regular overseas trips. She said that no matter what else went on in our lives, two things would always be her number one priority. They were my education and travel. So with that in mind, she made an unwritten rule that we'd travel together once a year. Most of our trips were to New Zealand but it remained a damn fine rule, I thought. I guess Mum's commitment to travel stemmed from Mum having loved travelling when she was young. She enjoyed telling me about how when she'd first left home she'd gone to Europe, working different jobs from one day to the next, free to go wherever the wind blew, she would say. That had been a time when visas and work restrictions weren't so rigidly enforced and flights were reasonably cheap. More than anything else, I think it was my mother's inability to recreate those old memories that ruined later holidays for her.

Finally, when we stopped travelling together once Mum had begun to think that the world was against her. For her it seemed as if every holiday we went on ended in some kind of 'disaster' and no matter how hard she tried, she couldn't give me the times she remembered so fondly. Thinking back, I guess she was right in part because every holiday we went on did end in some minor disaster, but I don't think the world had it in for her. To me the stuff ups and disasters were all part of the experience of leaving your home and going into the world to see what it had to offer. I was never really surprised when things didn't go to plan, and I wondered what she expected. You wake up in the morning in your bed at home, just the same as you have done every day before, and then many hours later you go to sleep again on someone else's bed on the other side of the planet. Some things were bound to go wrong, and they mostly always did.

In the early years, we travelled locally and when I think about it now I can understand why. She really had no way of saving and paying for many long-distance holidays. We were living on her sickness disability pension and some pay from the odd bit of house cleaning that she managed to find. Maybe she had some money saved from the years she worked like a banshee but probably it was just a matter of frugal living and prioritising expenses to save enough for our holidays. Other than my school fees and our holidays away, she hardly spent a cent. So it's no wonder that most of the overseas places I remember visiting were in fact a number of islands not too far off the coast of Australia. Our first ports of call were New Caledonia, Vanuatu and Fiji, and I loved all of them. But the strange thing is I don't remember Mum being there with me. I have photos so I know she was there, and since I was aged between four and six when we first travelled it's not possible that I went alone, but I genuinely have no memory of her being at any of those three places.

In New Caledonia we stayed at Club Med and I remember I spent my days in the child care 'fun land'. I would play with a much older boy, who might easily have been ten, and was fascinated by his stories of how his father would belt him when he was naughty. My mother never really hit me except out of pure frustration, so I was entirely confused as to how my newfound mentor couldn't simply avoid the punishment by just moving out of the way. He explained to me that his parents prevented him from doing such a thing because his mother would hold him until his father was ready with the belt. Struck by a brilliant plan, I suggested that he could jump over the belt by tucking his legs up under his body. Clearly, I had little idea of what it was like to be belted by one's father. Aside from these odd conversations, he and I had a great time together during our holiday at Club Med.

Vanuatu I saw from the back deck of an ocean liner where bananas would be hung for anyone to eat whenever they were hungry. I feel as if I never stopped eating them. I have no idea what my mother was doing the entire time we were on that boat, because my memories of that trip are lost in a haze of banana eating.

Our Fiji holiday was one of those island packages that included your own wicker bungalow, on an island of white sand you could walk around in twenty minutes. There was the 'unique' experience of a traditional 'cook-your-dinner-in-the-ground' as well as 'receive-a-necklace-of-flowers'. I remember one man broke his neck diving into a swimming pool and a helicopter came to the rescue. Another time someone spotted a giant octopus from a glass bottom boat and that night we ate calamari for dinner. I also recall befriending a local waiter named 'Milkshake' and that I was nearly assaulted. How I came to be in such a situation I can't remember, but I know I was hanging around with Milkshake out the back of one of the restaurants, sitting in a hut with some of the locals – and naturally my mother wasn't there. I remember lying on my back and being held down by several very large Fijian men as they tried to force a cigarette into my mouth. I was very afraid. Someone came in so they let me go and I shot out the door as fast as a rabbit. It may well have been innocent fun for them, but it really shook me up.

Decidedly less exciting trips for me were to good old New Zealand where I sometimes spent summers with my mother's family. By about the age of eleven I became quite accustomed to being dropped at the airport by my mother the required hour and a half before a flight and being left to fend for myself. I don't remember her ever hanging around until departure time. Now I can say with assurance that I am an experienced traveller – and the best way to travel is on your own. Airline staff are generally cautious about minors travelling unaccompanied by an adult so when I would arrive at the check-in counter, the first question would be, 'Where's your Mum?' Then I'd be whisked off and into the lap of luxury. I'd wait in the first class lounge until the flight took off, I'd have an attendant take me straight through all the customs areas and I'd be the last one on the plane. On landing, I'd be the first off, and it would be all smooth sailing through customs until I'd reach Auntie Jo, when suddenly I was just an ordinary person again. The best memories I have of international travel are from when I was under-age and travelling alone.

On one particular solo trip to New Zealand I was taken to a security office after I arrived at Brisbane airport. Just before the plane was due to take off there was an announcement over the airport intercom demanding that I report to the departures gate immediately. Looking back, I'm surprised that I even heard the announcement because I pay little enough attention these days, let alone when I was eight and living in my own childhood fantasy world. At that time, I was taken by two huge men from airport security back through the customs area where uneasy people looked on with sympathetic interest. We entered a room that could only be accessed through a door which had no handle, and I was very excited because my childhood fantasy world was coming alive. It seems there was another passenger named Damian Cooper, in a case of mistaken identity. The men asked me what seemed like hundreds of questions and delayed the plane until they were satisfied the situation was sorted out. So I was able to see James Bond-esque parts of the airport that most people never see, and all the while I was having the time of my life. I was eventually allowed to board the plane feeling a little guilty about everybody else on the flight being delayed.

The biggest adventures and the biggest dramas occurred when the holidays took me further away from Australia than just across the Tasman. During these trips to the United States and Europe, I can certainly remember my mother being present. Travelling overseas might be considered hazardous enough but it was especially so travelling with my mother. Her now frail constitution was just no longer up to the challenge.

I remember when I was about eleven I spent a horrible night with in a small dark hotel room in Portugal. At about one o'clock in the morning, I woke up and became very worried when a case of food poisoning that my mother had picked up from a local restaurant went from bad to worse. By this time Angie weighed less than forty kilos and I didn't know what to do. I felt all alone in a foreign country where I couldn't speak the language. I had dealt with life-and-death-call-the-ambulance situations with my mother before but those had been on home ground. This was a whole different thing. I was very relieved when she rang reception the hotel management took care of it. A doctor came and gave her some shots and then gave me a little talk based on the story I'd heard many times before about whether she'd get better, that is was 'touch-and-go'. Then he left, so I spent a very long night sitting up listening to my mother's breathing. The friends we had planned to meet the next day arrived for breakfast and immediately booked into the hotel for a few days until Mum was well enough to go on with our travel. The rest of our holiday in Portugal was excellent and I was young enough not to have been marred by its shaky start, but Mum forever wrote that one off as 'a disaster'.

It seems to me now that no child's experience of overseas travel is complete without at least one trip to Disneyland, and we went twice. Or I guess I should say that I went twice. For the first trip I must have been quite young because I don't really remember anything about it except that I had a wonderful time and always wanted to go back. So, being the indulgent mother of a single child, Angie set up another trip for me when I was about thirteen. The plan was for a stopover in Hawaii and then a hotel stay in Anaheim for a day-trip to Seaworld and, of course, tickets to Disneyland. We had only been off the plane for half an hour and hadn't even left the Los Angeles airport when Mum had her first *grand mal* seizure. I learned that in the United States when you put out a call for an ambulance you don't just get an ambulance, you also get the police and the fire department. It was very exciting, and the American accents meant that for me it was just like being on television.

After this experience I thought that maybe Mum was just interested in seeing how hospitals in other parts of the world compared with those at home, because for nearly the whole two weeks we were in the United States, Mum was on her back in a hospital bed. But that didn't stop me from having a good time because after spending a day and a half sitting in the hospital waiting room, I went home with a very kind nurse who'd offered to put me up at her place. It was a truly unique experience living with this apple pie, all-Spanish-American family and it offered me such a clear insight into the lives of average Americans. To this day I think of that family when I hear people generalising about Americans and I am grateful to have had that opportunity. The family would entertain me at night with their seventy something channels of television heaven, and during the day when they were at work and school I would visit Mum in hospital and then look after myself, including going on a series of one-day tourist bus trips. It took some convincing to get the bus driver to pick me up from the hospital but once I passed that hurdle it was all clear skies. I saw all the big attractions. Disneyland was a disappointment the second time around but Universal Studios more than made up for it.

When I think about it now, all that gallivanting around on my own seems so reckless. They say that knowledge is power but it works both ways. Knowledge is also debilitating. If I was living my childhood again, I don't know if I would now do the things I did back then – when I was too young to realise the dangers I was exposing myself to – even though nothing bad ever came of it. Mum, of course, classified that last trip to America as a monumental failure. After all, she spent most of the holiday in hospital. But I think back on it happily.

The times that I didn't like were the times when Mum would sometimes leave me in the hotel room to go out at night, and come home drunk. I hated my mother being drunk – it really scared me. I was afraid that when she was drunk she would start talking about things that we never talked about, things I never wanted to talk about ... namely, her *anorexia*. In retrospect, I see that it was really pleasurable for her to occasionally get drunk, and had I been old enough I probably would have joined her and we could have had a great time together. I hated her going out drinking but I can see now that it was not always a bad thing. One night in a hotel in Amsterdam when she was out drinking I had a wonderful time watching a succession of complimentary try-before-you-buy five minute bursts of in-house adult entertainment. Although I was upset when my mother drank too much, I don't mean to make it sound as if she was an alcoholic as it only happened a few times during my childhood.

All in all, my travel adventures, both with and without my mother, allowed me to discover that the world was an amazing and fun place for a kid with no agenda, few controls, and what seemed like a limitless supply of money. My experiences travelling when I was young were probably nothing like what my mother would have hoped for me. The travel reality certainly wasn't what she hoped for herself. But I learned a lot of interesting things: how to ask for a hot dog in Spanish; the difference between a household stool and the kind of stool a doctor wants to know about when confronted with a case of food poisoning; and how to shake hands with two one dollar bills folded in your palm. I think that maybe Mum was cursed by her own inability to focus on the positive and laugh at the negative, and her real undoing was her failure to see that despite all that happened, I mostly still managed to have a good time.

Chapter 6

Back at home and now moving into my early teens, I had come to realise how little my mother had to do with the day-to-day process of my growing up. In earlier years, partly by virtue of innocence and my own unwillingness to dwell on the negatives in my life, I had managed to get on with the business of being a kid pretty much on my own. This worked well enough in early childhood but as I stumbled into my teens, lots of question marks began jostling for space in my head, and life became more complicated. I had abandoned any idea that my life was like other kids' lives. Maturity had been thrust upon me in my earliest years and I realise now that this hampered me in some ways. I had trouble maintaining friendships with other children my age and when possible I sought out the company of adults or much older children. Mum's apparent disinterest in how I filled in my days became a characteristic to be exploited. I had already successfully navigated the first dozen years of life quite successfully so it might have been expected that an adolescence spent without anyone to rebel against should have been a breeze.

When I left the house on any given Saturday morning I would take my board, my bike, a bag of essentials, and go without telling Mum. Any information I gave her was on a need-to-know basis.

'Okay, Mum, I'm heading off,' I would say, not long after breakfast.

'Do you have some sunscreen on?'

'Yes Mum, and I have some more in my bag.' I had become more paranoid about getting sunburnt than she had.

'I'm going down to meet David and then I think we're going over to James's place to get a ride with his mum out to Point Cartwright. I'm not sure when we're going to be back.'

'Well, love, it's probably better that I don't know. As long as you're outside having fun then that's fine.'

'Sure. Well I'll call you if I'm not going to be home tonight, okay?'

'Alright, as long as I know whether or not I need to have something ready for your dinner.'

'Okay.' And with that I'd be gone.

Her logic was that if she didn't know where I was, or when I would be home, she would be less likely to worry if I was late or somewhere that she didn't want me to be. Although this probably wasn't the kind of logic that would withstand the scrutiny of a court's investigation, it seemed to work quite well for us. The only rule we had was for me to call home if I wasn't going to be there in time for dinner. It didn't matter where I was, it was just important that she knew if she had to cook or not.

I can only assume that my free-spirited adventuring, my unsupervised gallivanting, must have raised a few eyebrows and prompted a few hushed conversations among the other mums. Partly conscious of this fact, I made a mental note to try to spread myself evenly around the neighbourhood, never ending up at the same friend's family more then two weekends in a row. It would be easy to fool myself into thinking that things were different back then, that the world was a safer place and that my free-wheeling was not nearly as risky as it now sounds. Yet I never felt unsafe. I knew hundreds of faces from all over the coast, I knew the names of the local shop owners and, for instance, the old guys who only surfed Dead-Man's Bluff. I knew the house of a school friend in just about every suburb block. I knew all the old bush shortcuts and where the odd secret cubby house was located. In some ways it seemed as if I was negotiating the urban terrain with the same cunning and nous as a homeless city street kid. The difference was that I always had something of a home to return to.

***

It wasn't until I was well into my teens and about to go into Year 9 of high school that I started to make any lasting friendships. The year before, I had received an award for anti-social behaviour. Let me explain ... The school, Matthew Flinders Anglican College, opened for the first time in the same year that I started Year 8 and was built on what used to be an orange orchard. The school administration bulldozed only enough orchard each year to build any additional buildings needed at that stage, so in that first year there was enough of an orchard remaining for the school to make a little money selling oranges. As I had chosen to study agriculture that year, and did not feel a need to make new friends, I automatically found myself spending most of my free time in the orchard picking oranges. The school's response to my isolating behaviour was to give me a service award at the end-of-year awards ceremony. Even at that age, I thought it strange that the school would decide to reward my behaviour rather than encourage me to socialise. I guess now that there was a subtle message in the award aimed at encouraging me to socialise.

Although it never occurred to me at the time, I now wonder about how my mother was able to afford for me to attend that school. My year was always the highest year of the school while I was there, so we never had any older kids to bully us while all the younger kids were expected to look up to us. One negative was the school's need for funds, so on top of tuition fees the school regularly asked for a voluntary 'building contribution' of about five hundred dollars. This meant that when school fees were due Mum would give me a small wad of cash in an envelope to take to the administration building where I would regularly be quizzed as to why there wasn't enough money inside. I would then have to carefully explain that we, Mum and I, were not going to be able to pay the building contribution this term which was invariably followed by a certain amount of confused paper shuffling and glances over the shoulder by the receptionist who hadn't been authorised to handle such discrepancies.

Embarrassment over money matters notwithstanding, I did have a few friends come and go who were a funny mix of nerds and nobodies, the grey people who avoid interaction with all but their own kind. I probably fitted right in. Early on in the year I spent a few weeks living with a guy named Aaron and his family. Aaron was an awkward towering mass of a kid with big coke-bottle glasses and a wicked sense of humour, who had been admitted into the school on an academic excellence scholarship. Aaron's oversized body and its matching oversized brain were predominantly directed toward the study of firearms and all things macabre.

'Have you seen the first Robocop movie?' Aaron once asked me, as we lounged about in his littered bedroom at his place.

'Yeah, it's really a cool movie!' I say.

But I find Aaron isn't interested in my four star rating response.

'You know that bit at the start ...?' he asks. 'When they're testing the prototype version, the one with the big double chain Gatling guns?'

I look up to the ceiling, searching my brain to recall a significant scene.

'The bit right at the start when the executive guy gets blown out of the window by the robot?'

'Oh, yeah, yeah. I remember that bit.'

'Ok, so you remember the executive guy is asked to test the prototype Robocop by pretending to take someone hostage?'

'Yeah, and the machine stuffs up and won't stop threatening him even after he puts the guy down, right?'

Now I'm with you, Aaron, I say to myself.

'Do you know the make and model of the handgun the executive guy was holding?

And he loses me again.

I probably learnt more useless military paraphernalia from Aaron than I did in my ensuing years in the Army. Aaron played chess every night with his dad, a man who painted houses to feed his family but carried some unseen weight about his person that was suggestive of missed opportunities and unmet potential. His parents were good people, and when Aaron later left the school I missed him a lot.

To my absolute surprise I was invited to the birthday party of a boy named Greg which entailed being picked up from school by a stretch limousine and sampling the fine taste of Schweppes lemonade in tall thin glasses all the way home. It was a very agreeable experience and as it was my first group sleep-over party it has stuck in my memory. Greg's parents had a swimming pool and a billiard table which we all took full advantage of until late into the night when we retired into the slumber room to fall asleep, with Aaron regaling us with tales of woe. Despite these good times I was aware that I always remained on the outer edges of these friendships. I was nothing more than a member of a large social group, when what I really sought was something more personal. I never felt comfortable just being a group follower so in those early days I was always happier either at home, surfing, or doing my own thing somewhere else.

Despite this slow start, by the time I reached Year 9 I had a few friends and spent less time in the orchard, eventually forming my first strong friendship with two boys named Jackson and Cameron. Our mutual friendship quickly developed a kind of exclusivity and we each formed a sense of brotherhood, calling ourselves the 'Legendary Trio', and deciding that we needed nothing else in the world but each other. Because I went by bus to school I would usually arrive before the other two who were dropped off by their respective parents, so I would wait on my own in a small patch of scrubby forest that bordered the orange orchard. Jackson would show up first, his slight agile frame darting quickly through the trees toward me in a mock battle charge, stopping just short enough to release his school bag off his shoulder so that it flew at me like a weapon. We would kick around with each other, talking about something we had seen on television or some idea we had thought up the night before until we heard Cameron approaching. Cameron was the unspoken runt of the group which was not to say that we thought any less of him, simply that he was invariably the butt of all our jokes. As he approached, Jackson and I would hide below the light groundcover ferns with thin long sticks in hand until he was close enough, then out we'd charge into the fray, whooping and yelling. Later we'd each reluctantly disperse to our individual classes until morning tea time when we would once again meet up in our secret little wood and entertain ourselves with imagined *Lord of the Rings*-style adventures.

In Year 10 the three of us decided to form a gang of which we were the only members and into which no one else was invited. While a gang of three members seems rather pitiful to me now, we certainly didn't think so at the time. This was the kind of gang that required you to say that you were a member while you were at school, and then you were free to forget about it when you were at home. We were young middle class white kids duped by television into acting out romanticised ideals. In a school so small, little went unnoticed and so it soon transpired that some of the other boys, those on our social peripheries, had caught wind of our gang and formed one of their own.

'Who are you?' a boy named Mark randomly enquired one day.

'What?' I asked, rather confused.

'I said who are you?'

'What are you talking about, Mark? You know perfectly well who I am.'

'Yeah, but *who* are you, like who are you with?'

'I don't know, Mark ... *who* are you with?' I said with an edge in my voice.

'Hmph! Well, you're obviously not with us because we're the *Blue Tags* and if you're not with us then you're against us.'

Having finished his speech, Mark powered off to reunite with the other five kids in the mighty *Blue Tags*.

I made my way back to Jackson and Cameron who were waiting for me at our *Red Dragon* headquarters.

'Have you guys heard of the *'Blue Tags'*, because I just had a really strange run in with Mark who was carrying on like some weird secret squirrel?'

'Steve and Dave and some others have formed a gang called the *Blue Tags*,' Jackson explained.

'You're kidding!' I said.

'Nup. They asked us if we wanted to join and when we said no they started going on about there only being one gang in this school and that we either have to join 'em or fight 'em,' Cameron put in.

'Well, what are we going to do?' I asked, as I could see Jackson and Cameron had already been thinking about it.

'Well, that's up to them because we don't want any trouble but if they do then I'm just going to call over some other *Red Dragons* from Maroochy High to help us,' Jackson replied. He always had a solution at the ready.

It had been Jackson's idea to start the gang in the first place and he had picked up the plan from another friend of his who went to a public school. In reality we had no knowledge of another *Red Dragon* chapter at the public school. Even if there was, it's likely it only enjoyed the same level of groundswell support as ours – and that was none.

Nevertheless we emerged from our forest full of misplaced bravado so that during the following two days tensions mounted, voices were raised, and scuffles were exchanged until finally a showdown was arranged between the growing number of *Blue Tags* and the imaginary *Red Dragon Army*. Equally strangely – and I can see from this distance in time that it was predictable – somewhere between the time of arranging a date and the actual day of the showdown, everyone involved lost interest. The gangs dissolved without incident or remorse and school life returned to its normal humdrum. What remained was a unity forged between Jackson, Cameron and myself through our commitment to stand together, outnumbered and yet unmoved, against what for us at that age seemed like the rest of our world. The three of us remained bound in our friendship with each other until the very end of our schooldays.

While it must have been almost inevitable that I ended up living with Jackson and his family, I continue to think of it as a blessing that I did. This was the innocuous way it occurred …

I was having a conversation with Jackson one day about his old friend Aaron, who had briefly attended Matthew Flinders School, when I happened upon a curious piece of information.

'Do you still see Aaron at all?' I asked.

'Not much, he's at Maroochydore High now but I think his parents might be moving away soon. I don't know. They're funny kind of people.'

'I thought his parents had separated. Wasn't his dad a real bastard or something?'

'Yeah, Aaron came and stayed with us for a while when things were really bad,'

'Did he?' I interjected with a partly inquisitive and partly excited tone in my voice.

'Yeah, but then he went back to his mum who has now gotten back together with his dad so I don't know what's happening, but it's not good,' Jackson finished.

And with that I set the wheels in motion and to the delight of us both, it wasn't too long before I'd moved in with Jackson's family, sleeping on a pull-out mattress on the floor of his bedroom.

My life at this time seemed to be flowing in series of successively smooth steps. First, I had made new and meaningful friends. Next, although Mum was still physically unwell, she was more mentally stable. Then, to top things off, I began to entertain thoughts about girls! I started walking part of the way home from the school bus stop with a girl who lived a few doors away from my place. Louise was in a class a few grades below me and I had never entertained any ideas about a relationship with her until one lunchtime at school one of her friends approached me.

'Louise wants to know if you will go with her.'

Well of course I would, what else was I going to do, presented with an opportunity like that? There was no way I was going to say no.

'Okay,' I replied – and with that the deal was done.

Needless to say, walking home that afternoon with her was a little awkward. I was completely clueless. The only interaction that Louise and I had during the time we were going out was those walks home from the bus stop. This didn't seem to bother either of us and in all honesty I think we spoke less during the time we went out than when we were just friends. After about two weeks of this I was informed by another of Louise's friends that I had been dumped because she wanted to ask out another boy. I had bought her a Garfield key ring with her name written on his tummy but there was no love lost and I decided she might as well keep the key ring. Yet to my surprise later that same lunchtime her friend returned it to me so, not knowing any other girls named Louise, I put it in the bin. As it turned out, the other boy she had been chasing turned her down and so in true schoolyard romance fashion she asked me out again. I found it all too unusual and declined.

The following year I developed my first crush on a girl named Tracie. She was the sweetest thing I had ever seen, with her long wavy brown hair, big almond brown eyes, soft olive skin and an innocent playful personality. Tracie and I might never have spoken had we not been in the same drama class but with that small opportunity in my timetable and my determination that we would always wind up in the same work group together, we became good friends. Tracie was in what I considered the cool crowd, her core group of friends being the kids that had already discovered alcohol and serious dating. She would regularly tell me about their secret weekend exploits. But I had no desire to be part of that crowd and my friendship with Tracie probably stemmed from the fact that she was about as innocent as I was.

'Yuck, there's Michael,' she said, turning her back on him to face me.

'Why *yuck*?' I asked, only interested in why she thought he was repulsive as I had decided a long time ago that Michael, a rugby thug, school bully, and all round bastard was an arse.

'Michael got Lindy really drunk on Saturday night at a party at Sally's parents' house and he had his hand up her shirt in front of everyone. Then later he took her off somewhere and no one knows what they got up to. Guys are such pigs, Damian.'

'Yeah, Michael is.'

'What happened to just holding hands and all that stuff? You know, like in the Beatles song … *I wanna hold your ha-a-and* …'

Her voice was intoxicating and I sat there longing to be able to just hold her hand but I said nothing. The whole year we were friends I said nothing, and I wonder now if she knew how much I worshipped her. It's hard to imagine that she could have missed the signs. Our friendship ended at the end of Year 10 when Tracie decided to drop out of school and work for her father.

The end of Year 10 was a strange time at my school and I was particularly affected by the knowledge that this would be the end of my close friendship with Tracie. In our last week of school, after all our exams were finished and we were nothing more than inmates biding time until our release, we all made grand gestures of friendship. We would sit on the oval and sing songs to heightened emotion whenever someone brought in a portable stereo. We played Ben E. King's *Stand By Me* on loop until no one could cry anymore. Girls were wearing their boyfriends' shirts or swapping hats and ties, and everyone signed each other's shirts in big black felt pens.

Everyone wanted photos with this person or that. Even the teachers were compelled to join in, and still the tears flowed. I continue to have strange flashbacks to those last few days of Year 10 and seriously wonder if it all really happened. Over about four years that we had been there as the so-called leaders of the school, a kind of togetherness had unknowingly developed so that the impending end of Year 10 – when so many of our number would not be returning – suddenly seemed too much for us to take. So intense were the feelings, when our graduation came around two years later on our very final day of school at the end of Grade 12, it paled in comparison. It was as if in Year 10 we had been still just young enough to take the ideals of the television show, *The Wonder Years*, a little too much to heart.

Following Year 10, Tracie's and my friendship circles began to broaden and the final years of high school were about as normal for me as they were for anyone else. The legendary trio – Jackson and Cameron and I – remained extremely close friends, but we all started to meet a few other people as well. The problem for me at first was that Jackson and Cameron were both doing science-based subjects while I was doing arts subjects, so I was left with no choice but to interact with others. At the top of that list was a guy named Steve, who, like me, was taking senior drama. Steve was one of those people that you just can't help but like.

'Damo!' he would yell as I entered the drama theatre. No one called me Damo but somehow coming from Steve it was fine.

'Steve, you old dog!' I'd rise to his level of sociability.

'Miss Ridley's away today, did you hear that? So we're going to have a substitute teacher! A *substitute* teacher!' he says with a wicked grin.

'Steve, we're in Year 11, man, not Grade 6.' I use a pleading tone.

'Yeah, so? That's even better really because she won't be expecting a thing. ... Hi Megan.'

'Hi Steve,' Megan replies, sounding flirtatious, as she walks in and joins her friends at the other end of the room, with Steve watching her all the way.

He turns back to face me. 'God, she's hot. I think she's so hot,' he whispers.

'I know, Steve, I know.'

Steve was one of those people who had enough charisma to carry himself well just about anywhere and very often that charisma carried him directly into the arms of a wide selection of girls. He would regularly regale me with the details of his exploits, both current and previous, and on more than one occasion I was roped into the personal politics of his elaborate love life.

'Damian, were you with Steve on Saturday night?' Lindy asks me.

'Um...'

'Come on, either you were or you weren't ... You weren't, were you?'

I've never been able to lie in matters pertaining to the heart.

'He wasn't with Cathy if that's what you're getting at.'

'Are you sure?'

'I promise you that he wasn't. I wasn't actually with him so I can't tell you exactly what he was doing but I can guarantee he wasn't with Cathy. He's totally over her.'

'Are you sure?' Lindy asks again.

'I'm sure, Lindy. There is absolutely nothing going on between them,' I say.

'Thanks, Damian. You're always good to talk to.'

And so it went. Steve wooed them and I was good to talk to. Steve, the stud, and Damian, the good old, non-threatening nice guy. If I sound bitter I don't mean to be. I thoroughly enjoyed living my romantic life vicariously through Steve. It was safe, easy and highly entertaining.

Chapter 7

I also had a life outside of school. It began after the reign of *Space Invaders* and *Frogger* but before *Sega* and *Nintendo*. This was a time when video game machines in take-away shops were the most sought after things on the planet for young adolescent boys. In my neck of the woods, the arcade game craze all started with *Double Dragon*. It cost forty cents to play so I virtually lived down at the local Tenpin Bowling Centre. Like so many other local kids, I made that place my home away from home, specifically in the dimly lit, top right hand corner of the bowling alley where the six or so video game machines illuminated the relative darkness with their multi-coloured screens constantly flickering and changing colour. For us, it was more than just the place to play video games; it was our hang-out. We were the locals and we easily identified all the outsiders. Our names were on the scoreboards of every machine, even the boring car game with real steering wheels that no one was ever seen actually playing. Everything we did during those days revolved around acquiring yet another forty cents. Even a dollar wasn't a simple dollar value to us – it represented three games, because the deal was one game for forty cents or three games for a dollar. Even when we didn't have money, we would watch other kids play with their money and give advice to the obviously less experienced, while we kept tabs on our favourite superior players. These days didn't last forever. When we'd conquered one game another would replace it, and as our insatiable desire for new games grew, so did their price tags. Soon enough, games were a dollar a pop and we were out of the market.

This was when I got lucky. If I had watched this scenario unfold on my television on a Sunday night prefaced by an introduction from Walt Disney himself I wouldn't have been the least bit surprised. Around the age of thirteen, I became friends with a guy I'll call 'Tony', who was maybe not much older than twenty-one at the time which probably accounts for much of what might be described as juvenile behaviour. But in my mind he was a mature adult. As a result of some kind of family inheritance and presumably a keen business sense, Tony ran his own entertainment company. It offered modern and classic jukeboxes for hire and video games to buy or lease. Tony also performed a professional adults' or children's magician's routine. Whether Tony was twenty-one or forty-one years old, it meant the same to me back then and consequently I afforded him the same amount of respect and trust as I did any other adult male. Unfortunately, or perhaps fortunately, at his age and with that sort of financial independence, Tony didn't recognise the responsibility my trust bestowed on him, which meant our adventures pushed the boundaries.

The jukeboxes were Tony's bread and butter. The classic, old-style units he leased to pubs and clubs only required to be emptied of cash about once a month, but he would rent new CD players for private parties and functions on a nightly basis. This meant that most of his Fridays, Saturdays and Sundays were spent in his ute driving all over the Sunshine Coast delivering and picking up one-hundred-and-thirty-kilogram jukeboxes. Not an easy task for one person and probably quite lonely too. Enter Damian. Add one small pair of hands and an excitable spirit for adventure and you have a recipe for endless weekends of fun. Tony was a big guy and it would probably be fair to say that he could handle those jukeboxes quite well on his own so, in retrospect, I guess my job was mostly a morale boost for him.

Tony would phone my house out of the blue from his ute, parked a few kilometres away from my place, to explain that he had a pick-up and wanted to know if I was coming. He was the first person I knew with a mobile phone and I remember phoning my mother from the ute as Tony drove me away from the house. I gave her a detailed account of the shops we lived near as Tony and I drove progressively further away. It can't have been that exciting for her: 'Now we're going past this shop, now that shop, Mum.' But I knew that was the kind of information that would satisfy her.

Without a moment's hesitation I used to join Tony. I would cancel plans, abandon friends, and once or twice I even skipped school to rush downstairs with a backpack stuffed with a few essentials just in time to see him come round the corner. All this behaviour fell under the shaky umbrella of my mother's 'if he's out of the house then he's having fun' ethos.

The deliveries were fun enough, but it was really the activities that happened either side of a drop-off that kept me interested in spending my weekends hauling oversized stereos to people's houses. Tony never took me home after just one job. In fact, I don't remember him ever taking me home without my having to ask, so after a drop off it would be either on to another job or back to his house. At first he lived in a large high-set fibro house built on a large suburban block, with a rundown tennis court and a garage closed in to create a massive space. In that garage lived 'the machines': jukeboxes that weren't being rented as well as what I referred to as 'the gold', the video game machines that weren't currently in any take-away store or bowling alley. I loved it down there playing all those free video games all night, playing until my legs hurt from standing still for too long and my eyes could look only straight ahead without hurting.

Coca Cola once ran a competition that involved collecting a certain number of cans and the person with the most cans would win a CD jukebox. As the machines retailed at around fifteen thousand dollars, Tony figured he could win the competition by buying about eight thousand cans of Coke, effectively picking up a new jukebox for half price. I remember the day the pallet-loads of Coke were delivered to Tony's garage, and I remember the nights of no sleep, playing video games sustained by can after can of Coke. But I don't remember if he ever won that jukebox.

There was a world of fun to be found upstairs in Tony's house as well. As a professional magician he always had a wide range of interesting and bizarre toys and contraptions lying around the house. There was a massive lolly dispenser, the kind small children whine to their parents about in shopping malls. It was stocked with M & M's. He also had a large screen television wired to a jukebox for maximum audio output and a range of pirated movies for young and old. I was at a stage when I was very slowly beginning to formulate an understanding of sexual arousal. Tony, on the other hand, understood it only too well, and sought only to satisfy. My vision was burst wide open as I ventured my way into his expansive collection of porn videos, novelties, games, magazines and the unrelenting sexual innuendo that was a permanent part of any conversation with Tony. During the years I spent visiting Tony's house, the balance of time I spent between upstairs and the garage downstairs shifted sharply from mostly down to always up.

Despite Tony's vivacious sexual frustration, there was always sufficient hint in the air of a willing woman so that nothing untoward ever happened between us. As an adolescent, the notion of the possibility of sexual relations between us never occurred to me, nor to him, I presume. I realise now that I was very fortunate that Tony was as trustworthy as he was. I don't mean to cast any negative aspersions on Tony at all. Rather, I realise that many times I put my trust and my safety in the sphere of older men in general, men I did not know and would have been powerless to escape from should the need have arisen. There is no doubt that my desire to find a loving male role model led me into some precarious situations, but I'm thankful that through luck, my own common sense, and the concern of other men, no harm ever came to me.

While in Tony's house I struggled to shake off my boyish desires and adolescent curiosity. Outside, on the road, the limited responsibilities Tony afforded me filled me with feelings of importance and confidence. When we picked up a jukebox it was my job to open it and remove all the CDs and get it ready for transport while Tony sorted out the account. We cleared the coins from dozens of video game machines up and down the coast, in and out of all the old take-away stores that had not so long ago been my daily haunts. Key in hand, I would kick other kids off machines mid-game to clear the coins out and then I would ring them up a few credits just because I could. Back in the car, I would take the wheel whenever Tony got a mobile phone call or I would change the gears while he ate his McDonalds meals as he drove. We had a CB radio in one of the utes and I would try to pick up information about police traps from truck drivers in the local area. It was mostly an unsuccessful venture but good fun just the same. On our way home, Tony would often phone a pizza shop many kilometres ahead and close to home while I took the wheel. He would order two of his favourite pizzas to be picked by 'Jones'. An hour and a half later when we made it home, we would drop by the pizza shop and ask if there were any cheap pizzas going. And what do you know? There always were. At the time, Tony's philosophy that cold pizza at half the price was just as good as hot pizza seemed reasonable to me.

We didn't always end up going home after a delivery. Depending how close we found ourselves to

Brisbane, we would sometimes push on through the city to where Tony's sometime-business-partner lived. Tony and Roger worked together to try to get a number of video game arcades up and running. The genius of their plan was considered to be the combining of Tony's game knowledge and connections with Roger's local presence and management skills. As with most genius plans it never amounted to much and most of the time Tony and I would just show up to remove a few failing machines, which we'd take to some nearby fish and chip shops where we knew they would bring in more money. The business discussions all happened in Brisbane because that was where the American and Japanese video game machine importers had their showrooms and where the buying and selling, the wheeling and dealing, was done. It was an exclusive industry then and nothing was bought at full price when people knew people and the trading of machines was preferable to paying cash. So Tony would bargain and I would disappear into the showroom where all the newest and most ground-breaking machines were available for free play to the kid who had the ear of a big name buyer on the north coast.

Trips to Brisbane were always great and trips to the showroom were even better, but when a Brisbane trip went south, heading towards the Gold Coast, I knew I was en route to a bitter-sweet time. In Brisbane, Tony would buy and load onto the ute the latest gun-held shooting game which, before it was even on the ute, had been sold to a guy on the Gold Coast for two classic *Pac-mans* and a *Miami Vice* pinball machine. So we would go on down and make the trade. By now I wouldn't have been home in a day and a half and I'd be thinking that I should really bring more clothes on these trips. It was never a question of whether or not we would go. Even if there had been some kind of debate, my say wouldn't have counted for much because whenever he happened to find, or make, a reason to go to the Gold Coast, Tony's true destination was the casino. There was no arguing with that. He was a 'Black Jack' man. I say 'was' because I don't know him anymore so he may well still be. But I hope not, because in the time I knew Tony it was only ever the casino that detracted from his otherwise happy life.

Since, at that time, I was much too young to join Tony at the tables, I would be awarded a petty cash allowance to help while away the hours that Tony would spend on the other side of the bright carpet, flashing lights and conspicuous security personnel. Tony would go in with the pager and I would keep the mobile phone so that I could page him if I needed anything (such as more money to amuse myself). He would phone me on the mobile when he needed me (for instance, if ran out of money) and while he played 'Black Jack', I would answer the mobile and take messages so that he would not be disturbed. He was a gambling addict at that stage of his life, in my opinion. He would leave me with hundreds of dollars so he couldn't spend the kitty but, unable to stop himself, he would phone me to meet him to retrieve it when he had run out of his initial stake. He always thought he could win it back, but he never did. He always said at the end of the night that he had won but that never happened, at least not when I was with him. He would play until nearly all the money ran out. Sometimes he would keep enough for us to spend the last few hours before dawn in a boulevard strip all-night motel. Other times we just slept, or tried to sleep, in the car.

While Tony gambled, I lived it up. I had terrific fun during the hours he would spend in the casino, and I was too young to be concerned about him having any kind of gambling problem. He was an adult, so I trusted and obeyed. I could never go too far away because he might need me, and besides, if you lose enough money in the casino they will give you a free meal ticket for their restaurant so I never wanted to be too far away in case I missed the free feed. Fifty dollars was my usual allowance money when Tony went into the casino. If he was 'up' and phoned me to collect his winnings to hold, he usually gave me something extra. But I only ever counted on the original fifty to get me through the night. These days, on the opposite side of the road to the casino, is an enormous shopping centre. But when I was running around those streets with a fifty in my hand and a mobile in my pocket, the nearest thing to the casino was a brothel.

About two kilometres from the casino, seemingly in the middle of nowhere, there was a four-cinema complex and a Sizzler restaurant. This was nearly always my destination. A movie followed by an extended all-you-can-eat Sizzler experience, followed by another movie, would take care of the longer part of a casino binge session. Walking back to the casino after the last movie had finished was the only part of the night I was scared of. I tried to think of it as if I was a character from one of the game machines under Tony's house. I would have to battle my way down the spooky unlit Gold Coast Highway, then I would have won when I'd finally reached the casino, and the game would be over. The alternative was to miss the late movie by heading back to the casino while there were still a few people about. That meant I would have to spend a few extra hours in the casino lobby or the ute. So I always tried to stay for the late movie and suffered with my fear on the road late at night because I hated waiting so long at the casino.

When I did go back early, I would wander around the casino hotel or ride on the monorail that linked the casino with a high rise hotel on the other side of the highway. I never tried to sleep because I knew I couldn't. In the ute I would listen to music for a while but I was always paranoid about running the batteries flat. Today there are signs in the casino car park warning that it is an offence to leave children in the car. Not back then. In the early hours of the morning, mostly I just sat outside the casino entrance aimlessly watching people in the lobby and playing pretend *Keno* in my mind.

We were lucky that nothing ever happened to me on those nights. While I paint a fairly grim picture now, I remember the trips as being mostly fun and sometimes boring. There were never any words of caution or control that I remember, yet many people around me – friends, teachers, my mother's friends – surely knew because I must have bragged about it all, ever so proud of myself. I can't remember if Mum knew or not but if she did, she never spoke to me about it and she never stopped me from going out with Tony. I do remember that Ian and Rachel, who I'd known since I was about ten, were the first to first alert me to the fact that Tony's gambling might be a problem. For them to have mentioned it, I must have told them something of what was going on even though I was normally careful about what I told them. It's a wonder to me that nothing was ever said or done about it. It was Ian and Rachel who introduced me to Tony in the first place through some kind of church connection, I think. Ironically, it was partly because of them that I finally stopped hanging out with him.

Ultimately Tony and I just moved on from each other. He went on to buy a normal house in a tidy suburb, which still had a garage full of jukeboxes, but it was a normal-sized garage and he no longer had an 'upstairs'. He met a girl on the internet, which at the time was almost unheard of. But with Tony, being Tony, no one really batted an eye and he married her.

I'd left school by then and had moved to Brisbane, only seeing him on very rare occasions, mostly at night clubs where he used to sell magician's balloons which he would blow up and contort into a range of shapes. We would say 'Hi' in an awkward kind of way, he would blow me up a balloon free of charge, usually in the shape of a penis to wear on my head, and that would be the extent of our encounter. I would sit sporting my new penis, watching Tony make his way around the room before he moved on to the next night club. All the while I wondered if he ever knew what a significant and joyous character he'd been in my life.

***

I left home on the week of my seventeenth birthday. It had been over a year since Mum had been in hospital, so moving out felt like progress for both of us. I had been accepted into a nursing degree at Griffith University in Brisbane so I moved down before the course began in order to familiarise myself with the city. As everything I had I was able to fit into the back of Mum's car, we were able to deliver me neatly into my new life in just one trip. Mum didn't stay any longer than it took her to have a cup of tea, unceremoniously leaving me to unpack and get on with the business of being me, now on my own.

I lasted about six months. My nursing ambitions stemmed from a desire to be an ambulance officer, having been inspired by their kind and humanitarian work so many times in the past. But barely seventeen and having already dealt with my fair share of crisis and pain, I decided that nursing was not for me at that time in my life so I withdrew from the course.

I felt that I needed a break from concerns about health. I needed to do something completely different. Although I'd enjoyed my time socially at university, I lacked any kind of academic direction or enthusiasm so the thought of simply moving into another area of study did not appeal. I considered travelling abroad, following in the footsteps of my mother by getting odd jobs and taking opportunities as they arose. I had no money for an overseas airline ticket and no car for a domestic adventure. I made some flyers that said: *'young man seeks sail to anywhere, will work for passage and board'*", which I advertised around the local yacht marina but I didn't get any response. I was getting restless. I moved back in with Ian and Rachel for a while and got a job at the local Woolworths supermarket working afternoon and nights shifts in the fruit and vegetable department. I must have shown some promise because I was offered a place in the manager training program which I took no time in turning down. It was then that I decided to join the Army.

A program running at the time called 'The Ready Reserve Scheme', aimed to increase the Army's pool of well-trained reservists. You signed up for a period of one year full-time service followed by five years part-time during which period you'd be paid a living allowance equivalent to the government's 'Austudy' program. It seemed to meet my needs perfectly. A year away from everything and everyone I knew would be an experience unlike any other I would encounter later in life, and it didn't require me to be indoors with my face in a book. Following a lengthy and at times humbling selection process, I received my notification of acceptance a couple of days before Christmas in 1995. It was the last Christmas I would spend with Angie.

Chapter 8

Less than five months later, there I was sitting in a window seat on a Melbourne to Sydney flight, the first leg on my journey to the Sunshine Coast to say goodbye to my dying mother. By the time the plane was in the air, it was dark outside so there was nothing to see through my window. The plane was only half full and fortunately the seat next to me was empty. I was still wearing my Army camouflage uniform, which did nothing to help me blend into the beige interior of the aircraft. I reclined my seat, closed my eyes, and put a do-not-disturb expression on my face as I let my thoughts wander through the events of the last few hours and my mother's impending end. It seemed hard to imagine that her life might soon be over. After all the years of near-misses and maybes, the idea of Angie actually being gone from my life was almost inconceivable. I thought back to only a week and a half earlier when Ian and Rachel had come down to the base in Puckapunyal where I was stationed to attend my graduation march out parade. At that time, my mother's health had been the furthest thing from my mind because the Army parade was a big event in my life. I was to receive an award for being the 'Most Outstanding Soldier' in my platoon and, more generally, the parade marked the end of my Army recruit training and signified that I was now a soldier. It had been an arduous experience and I was completely self-absorbed in my own achievement.

Ian and Rachel flew down to attend as a show of support and to spend a few days in Melbourne sightseeing. Mum had decided not to come. She had given up on flying at the end of her last failed holiday, and she didn't really want to face all the people that would be there. Which was fine with me. The parade went off without a hitch, I received my award, and Rachel took lots of photos to take home and show Mum. After the parade, I had a day or two off from Army commitments and I spent that time with Ian and Rachel in Melbourne, visiting the Queen Elizabeth Markets and the Melbourne Zoo. They were staying in a bed and breakfast somewhere in Toorak so I spent a night there with them to save driving back out to Puckapunyal. In the morning, while Ian remained in their room reading the paper, I had a conversation with Rachel, clear in my memory as it took place in a sunroom with a bay window.

'Damian, are you upset at all that your mum didn't come down for the parade?' Rachel began.

'Um ... no, not really" I replied, not having thought too much about it. People often asked me questions about how I felt about my mum and I rarely gave my answers much consideration.

'I guess it would have been nice if she could have come, but I didn't expect that she would,' I added.

'She wanted to, you know.'

'Sure,' I said, starting to feel like I was being prepped for something.

'Yeah, she really did. She's so proud of you, you know that, don't you?'

'Yeah, I do. She always has been.'

'I know,' said Rachel. There was a silence. We looked at each other. Her discomfort was rubbing off on me and it began to feel annoying. I felt my mother's presence was once again imposing on my life, detracting from what should have been a day of excitement and simple sightseeing.

'Damian,' Rachel began, 'I want to ask you something about your mum.'

'Ok,' I said.

'How would you feel if your mum died? ... Um, no, that's not really what I meant to ask. I'm not sure how to put this Damian.'

'OK.'

'Do you think ... do you think you would be happier if she died, or, or would you prefer her to go on living?'

I didn't answer right away. I wasn't sure what she was asking. I shifted backward in my seat, moving slightly away from her. I was no longer concerned about her feeling of discomfort. Now my own feelings were much too strong.

'Is that it? Is that the question?' I asked.

'Yes. Yes it is,' she replied.

'Um ...' It was a tremendously hard question to answer. I sensed the importance of it, and while I suspected that my answer would reflect the type of man I was becoming, I was determined to answer truthfully.

'However I answer this, I feel like I'm being selfish,' I eventually offered. I thought some more, fidgeting uncomfortably in my seat and feeling dejected.

'On the one hand I think it would be better if she wasn't here anymore, I mean I know she would probably be happier if she wasn't here anymore. But then I wonder if I'm just saying that because I know how much of a burden she is on my life.' I paused, dropping my head to my hands and breathing deeply.

'But then again, if I say I want her to live, well then I'm being selfish for not letting her be free from it all. Why should she have to suffer?'

I didn't feel as if I was going to cry but I felt Rachel put her hand on my shoulder.

'What do you want?' she asked.

'I want her to live. I love her Rachel! I want her to be around for as long as possible, and I don't care what that means for me,' I said.

***

Now, just ten days after the conversation, Angie was dying – or as I thought of it, close to being dead. When we'd talked in Melbourne, Rachel hadn't made any judgements, she had just listened. But as my thoughts continued to wander, I considered the possibility that Rachel had known then that Mum was dying. I also wondered about how hard it must have been for her not to have tried to influence my decision or offer any kind of response or remark at the end of it. As for me, I was feeling a degree of relief. I was relieved that I had been able to answer honestly that I had wanted her to live; because if I had decided on the other alternative, and she'd died so soon afterwards, I might have been racked with guilt.

From the time of that fateful phone call on the Army parade ground to boarding the plane in Melbourne, my memory of events is vividly clear, but after that my memory is a montage of disconnected flashes. Somewhere between leaving Melbourne and arriving on the Sunshine Coast, Mum did pass away. It was no surprise. I found out from Ian and Rachel when I arrived on the Sunshine Coast. I do remember making a phone call to Emma, one of my dearest friends, from a pay phone in Sydney airport while changing planes.

Emma was the only person in the world I felt I could confide in. She'd been my first girlfriend, my first real love. Our relationship began in the final weeks of high school and we were intensely connected for the whole summer holiday, before I went off to university and she went to Japan for a year on a Rotary exchange trip. My relationship with Emma had introduced me to the idea of love without hurt. Even as an immature adolescent love, it gave me an experience of an unselfish generous trust in another human being. Emma and I broke up during her stay in Japan, so we were only together for less than a year, most of that time physically separated, but we remained very close friends.

My phone call to Emma was overwhelmingly emotional. Standing at the pay phone in a public thoroughfare in the terminal, I felt as alone there, amid the flurry of faceless commuters, as in the emotional void that was the Army. But at least there in the airport I was able to reach out. I took up the phone, pushed back the loneliness, and reached out to connect with a person who could help, to a place where my heart would feel safe. There was one person in the world who I trusted would give me understanding and empathy.

'Hello?' a kind familiar voice answers.

'Emma?'

'Yes. Who is this?' Her voice has changed from its normal vibrancy to hushed concern. 'Damian … is that you?'

'Yes.' I breathe my reply. Hearing her voice is like having a warm blanket thrown over my shoulders. At first just high school friends, our relationship had grown and intensified as the years passed.

'You sound terrible, Damian. Is there something wrong? Where are you?' she asks.

'I'm in the Sydney domestic airport. The Army is flying me home.' Tears roll down my face and my voice is broken and weak. I press my body as deeply as I can into the phone booth, trying to avoid the prying eyes of passers-by.

'Emma … my Mum has died,' I say. It's the first time anyone has spoken the words out loud and although an official pronouncement has not been made, I know it must be true by now. I've been thinking about her death since the phone call, but hearing it the words out loud makes them seem more real, and more painful.

'I'm so sorry.' I know her words are the best anyone can do in the situation.

I realise now that the anonymity of the public airport concourse, and the separation of Emma via the phone allows me the emotional sanctuary to completely break down. I drop my guard and cry uncontrollably. Emma listens, occasionally offering words of support but mostly just listening as I let eighteen years of pain, stoicism and compassion wash down my face onto the floor of Sydney airport. I stay on the phone with Emma until it's time for me to board my flight. She promises she will fly up to visit me the following day. I ask her if she will come to the funeral with me and sit next to me. She says that she will.

I loved my mother and I can feel the hole left behind by her absence already. I need someone else to love, to help me get through. Emma was easy to love.

Ian and Rachel, greet me an hour later at the Sunshine Coast airport hugging my body with an all-consuming embrace. They wrap their arms around me and hold me tight. They tell me that Angie has died in bed a little over an hour before. I accept the news without a flinch. In my mind I have already understood this, and in my heart I have already let go. They ask me if I want to go and see her body, to say goodbye, but I choose not to. I feel that I want to remember her just as I have always done. I want to remember her quick smile and her crystal clear green eyes. I know my real motivation behind not wanting to see her now is that I'm afraid to face a reality many times more powerful than I've talked about in my phone call to Emma.

On reflection, I realise that not seeing her body helped me to feel nothing for a long time after she died, by holding on to an idea that nothing much was different. For months after my mother's death, life seemed to be so much more manageable as I held onto the self-deluded notion that nothing had really changed even though Angie wouldn't be on the end of the phone anymore and had stopped writing letters. I had never really seen much of her anyway; the only difference now was that I saw nothing at all of her. Today I'm sorry that I didn't take up Ian and Rachel's invitation to view my mother soon after her death. I wish I had had something tangible to apply my grief to, something definitive to mark my ultimately finite relationship with my mother.

The last time I was with Mum before she died was on a three day leave from the Army, just over a month before her death. It coincided with what was probably the most intense period in my three-month basic training program. There had been a delicate shift from being given orders because we reservists were considered to know nothing, to orders that were loaded with expectation. We were (or at least some of us were) becoming soldiers, and as our proficiency to function in the military world grew, so too did the berating. When all the intimidation tactics of angst and punishment had passed and the threat of not going on leave had been vanquished by our actually being on board flights going home, we were elated. Those three days off were a roller coaster mix of the euphoria of freedom, and an ever-present trepidation about returning home. Like all my mates, I was hell bent on maximising every minute of my leave. Somewhere in the midst of my carousing, I managed to squeeze in a visit to Mum.

I found her at home in bed 'taking it a bit easy' and having 'not such a good day', but on the whole she assured me she was fine. I made us both a cup of tea and then sat on the side of her waterbed as I had done so many times before, feeling comfortable and at home in our private space. I thought of the many rainy days I had spent with her in that room and in that apartment, having convinced her to let me stay home from school, playing Scrabble and drinking tea. On the side of her bed, I recounted my stories of the Army training to her like a battle-weary hero returned from war. And in many ways that was what I was in her eyes, a soldier or a prince with a shield and sword, ready to go out to fight, to be strong in a world where she couldn't go. She listened to my stories with the same expression of profound admiration and pride that she had always used. I remembered that there had been times when I had found that unconditional love and admiration patronising; when it had felt that it didn't matter what I did because she would always be proud of me. Sometimes I had dismissed it as a maternal necessity. I had felt that because of her failings in life, anything I did seemed praiseworthy – and in part I was right. At the time it made me feel as if her praise was hollow and meaningless. But as I sat with her that day, I realised that my mother genuinely saw something special in me. I think she had always seen something in me that went beyond a mother's love for her child, that went beyond the fulfilment of her own life's failings. She saw a unique and strong human being worthy of her admiration.

'I love you,' she said softly mid-way through one of my stories, squeezing my hand gently to emphasise her point.

'I love you too, Mum,' I replied with a smile. I stroked the back of her hand with my free hand and studied it. It was the hand of an old woman, yet my mother was only forty-three. Her hand was thin and frail, the skin blotched and red, but it was also soft and familiar. I leant down and kissed it gently.

'I love you too.'

Then, as I sat with her, overfilling her ocean of pride in me with stories of the Army and impending manhood, Mum suddenly lapsed into an epileptic *grand mal* seizure. It's the sort of thing that can happen at any time and whether or not it would have happened if I hadn't been there I don't know. My feeling is that if it had, and I had not been there, it's likely she would have died alone some time later that day or the next day as medical staff may not have found her in time to save her. She was so frail by that stage that without immediate assistance, I think it's likely she would have faded away. As it was, I protected her from herself until the seizure had passed, then put her into a stable position and called an ambulance. At the time my feelings were not concern or fear, but more selfish feelings – disappointment and frustration that once again my mother had managed to infiltrate her needs into my time.

I stood around chatting with the ambulance officers as they loaded her into their wagon. They recognised me from previous encounters. Then I followed behind in Mum's car to the hospital. I stayed with her for a couple of hours, once again sitting on the side of her bed. This time it was a hospital bed and I was the only one drinking tea. My frustration at being held back from a desperately needed euphoric freedom grew by the minute. Finally I left, making an excuse about visiting a nearby friend's house, saying my goodbyes and explaining that I only had limited time and needed to be with other people. I'm sure she understood. I don't look back on that time and wonder if I left her feeling abandoned, because she was always very selfless in that way, but I try to imagine what I might have done if I had imagined that would be the last time I would ever see her alive.

At her death, that hospital scene was the memory that I chose not to replace with a viewing of her deceased body. The Army had given me ten days off for compassionate leave, a period considered just enough time to come to terms with a major loss in my life, to organise a funeral and to make arrangements for the handling of the remaining estate. The day after I'd arrived on the Sunshine Coast, Ian and Rachel took me to Mum's apartment. For some reason I was surprised by the fact that it all looked exactly the same. Her bed even had the same pale blue striped linen on it from the last time I had seen her. I couldn't bring myself to imagine that she had died in the bed less than twenty-four hours before. Someone had made the bed after she had been taken out, so that everything seemed completely normal. The only thing that seemed out of place to me was the number of people there. I remember having a slightly uneasy feeling that Mum would come home at any moment and be anxious and distressed by the people in her house. I remember there were a lot of strangers coming and going during those couple of days spent arranging things in Mum's old apartment, but mostly it was just Ian, Rachel and me there.

I spent some time with Mum's telephone address book finding the names and numbers of her friends and people she had been working for, and calling them to give them the news of her death. It might seem strange, but I derived a great deal of pleasure from doing this. Perhaps it was cathartic in some way. Whatever the reason, I relished the opportunity and was annoyed whenever people I phoned had already heard the news via some unofficial grapevine. The funeral director came with his glossy brochure full of photos of caskets to talk about when and how much it was going to cost to cremate my mother's remains. This interaction provided yet another minor disappointment as I childishly proclaimed to the man that my mother wanted to be cremated in the cheapest coffin I could find, 'preferably a cardboard box if possible'. These were her words, I told him. The smugness was wiped from my face as he responded to the comment, no doubt as he had done many times before, by flipping to the back page of his catalogue and stating, 'Then you'll be wanting the classic Brentwood, which is currently priced at three thousand dollars ...'

***

Among all those phone calls being made from Mum's all-in-one kitchen-dining-living room table – with her mishmash of assorted personal phone books and various scraps of paper strewn across it – an unsuspecting caller made his way into our insular world.

'Hello, this is Damian,' I responded into the handset.

'Yes, good morning, this is Jack Slater from the ANZ bank. Would Angela Cooper be available, please?'

'No, I'm sorry, she's not. Was it something important?' I played innocent while I felt myself slowly reeling him in.

'Ms Cooper has an appointment with me tomorrow afternoon and I was just phoning to confirm that she was still right to make that time,' he replied.

'Well, I don't think she is going to be able to make that meeting with you tomorrow, Mike, because she died two days ago.' … '*Badda boom! How do you like that slap in the face, buddy?*' I thought.

'Oh, oh …,' he eventually managed to stammer. I felt nauseous yet delighted at the unease in his voice, and offered no verbal lifeline for him to grab onto as he floundered in his own discomfort.

'… Well, I guess she won't be coming then.'

'No, I really don't think she will be.'

The other people in the room were looking at me with vague concern though I'm not sure whether it was directed toward me or the hapless soul at the end of my long fishing line.

'Um ... Well, I'll cancel that appointment and thank you for your time.'

'You're welcome, Jack. Have a nice day,' I said in conclusion with a hint of sarcasm.

Although no one said anything after I hung up, I had no trouble realising how childish my behaviour was. The thrill of the moment that had motivated my behaviour passed very quickly, and as I looked around the room at the others who were busying themselves with other things, I desperately felt the need to apologise. I think that I wasn't accustomed to feelings of childishness or remorse, because I'd played the role of mature and responsible adult for so many years, never allowing myself indiscretions of ignorance. Yet now things were different and at that moment I felt as though I had just lived my most genuine response to my mother's death since the whole thing began. For the first time in my life I felt the yoke of responsibility beginning to lift from my shoulders. I didn't like the feeling of being rude or childish any more than I liked being overly responsible. I had no desire to regress into volatile teenage-hood, but it felt good to finally be free. To be free as an adult.

Ian suggested that I might want to go over the road to the doctor's surgery and say thank you to the GP who had taken such a personal interest in Mum's health during the last few weeks of her life. I had met Dr Weedon once before, following a particularly impressive mountain bike accident, in which I had managed to rotate my arm in much the same way as I used to with my GI Joe army figures in order to pop their arms free from their bodies. My only other connection with the doctor had been in my teenage years when I'd coveted his black Porsche Carrera that I regularly watched him drive, in and out of his surgery carpark, from my old bedroom window.

I briefly explained who I was to the receptionist, saying that I hoped to meet briefly with Dr Weedon to say thank you. Ian made no attempt to interject, leaving me to choose my own words. We took a seat in the waiting room with the other handful of hopefuls, feeling slightly out place in not nursing a bandage or lolling a congested head. I noticed that from the inside of the waiting room I could make out the two back windows of Mum's apartment, and I wondered how many times Dr Weedon had stood in the same place looking up to wonder how Mum might be doing in the darkness that lay within. We hadn't been waiting more than five minutes when Dr Weedon came out and took us back into his office. He had no manila folder in his hand, yet he knew straight away who we were. Inside his room with the door closed, all seemed perfectly normal; it was cool with no windows, walls painted a deep blue, and a bed and assorted instruments and anatomical posters positioned around the place.

I introduced myself and worked my way around to thanking him for the extra care and attention that he had shown my mother. I had thought that I might just as easily have sent a card had his surgery not been so close. At a certain point as I noticed myself speaking the words of a Hallmark condolence card, he broke down and began to cry. I sat in a state of shock while he wept. He hadn't spoken a word since we'd come in and now I, too, had no idea what to say. Perched on his desk was a small collection of framed photos of his wife and two small boys. I looked at these and then at him and for the first time I saw him not as the omnipotent doctor conjured by my imagination, but as a very real, hurting and caring human being. Eventually Ian stood up and indicated to me that we should leave. Drawing myself up out of my chair and my confused oblivion, I walked out with Ian, leaving Dr Weedon in the privacy of his office. I've never seen or spoken to him again, but I have never forgotten the profound impact his moment of vulnerability left on me.

The experience with Dr Weedon was only a temporary injection of emotional realism into what was for me an experience more akin to a military manoeuvre than a period for expressing loss and grief. Over the course of that week, Mum's apartment was transformed into my campaign headquarters: Ian, Rachel and whoever else I encountered were converted into my foot soldiers; the apartment, the Sunshine Coast and anywhere else Mum had been was now my battleground. My mission was to eradicate all evidence of her existence from my life, my goal being not to forget about her, but to finally be able to live my life free from her demands. Disposing of her body was the first manoeuvre – and I considered that to be easy. The man, my soldier from the crematorium, would see to it. On my war phone, I had invited everyone I could think of to attend the funeral so they could say their goodbyes, in the hope that they would never again need to enquire about her to me. And, finally, I was making plans to have all of her belongings removed by the people in my logistics department, those who refer to themselves as pawnbrokers. I wanted everything gone. I wanted to be able to start afresh. Not just to end a chapter but to close the whole book of her life and begin writing a new book of life for myself. I had no feelings of animosity, my acts of cleansing were not vengeful, and I did not believe I was trying to shut out any feelings of pain or loss that I was experiencing. I simply wanted to be able to move forward with a clean slate. When she was alive she would, from time to time, say that she was holding me back from being truly happy, that her life prevented me from living my life. Although I dutifully disputed it then, her words rang loud and true as I planned to forge a new life for myself so soon after her death.

Chapter 9

I bought a suit, the first I'd ever owned, in order to impress at the funeral. It was a three-piece number, made from ash-grey micro-fibre, a material that hangs like silk but feels like satin, making it cheap and stylish at the same time. I wondered how many other young men had found themselves in a similar position, being measured for their first suit under such odious circumstances. Hiring a suit had seemed fine for the end-of-year school formal, but to do so for my mother's funeral just didn't seem right. The outfit cost me a little under five hundred dollars which was considerably more than I had ever spent on any item of clothing. In fact it came close to being the most I had ever spent on anything. It felt significant. I walked out of the shop with my three-piece suit neatly folded in an oversized glossy cardboard bag with string handles, and I got a sense of being a man. Things were changing for me: the way I was interacting with others; the way I thought about life. Everything felt different. I was no longer my mother's son, and I felt that I never would be again.

A couple of days before the funeral service, in the middle of the planning and preparations, I drove down to Brisbane for one night to visit my aunt, Chris. She lived at Manly in Brisbane's east, overlooking Moreton Bay, and she had my grandmother, Bette, and my aunt, Jo, staying with her. They had both come over from New Zealand for the funeral, and it was the first time either of them had been over to visit Angie – not because they hadn't wanted to but because Angie wouldn't let them. But now Angie had no choice in the matter. It was an incredibly awkward time being with all of them. I felt as if I was on some kind of diplomatic mission to represent Angie and somehow apologise for her past and present wrongs. Mum had never been comfortable with her family. She was never very comfortable with anyone, but the feelings of self-doubt, loathing and worthlessness brought on by her anorexia were always intensified when she was with her family. The years of constant separation from them developed, in my mind, a kind of 'us-versus-them' mentality. As a result I felt a small sense of betrayal that night, as we all had dinner at a restaurant. I felt as if I was double-crossing everyone, yet I didn't stop for a moment to consider how they might be feeling.

Later that night back at Chris's house, my grandmother and I sat talking alone in the lounge room, each of us drinking a cup of tea, in good English fashion. Bette seemed worn down. The pain of her daughter's death and the events of the day had taken their toll. Old age was finally catching up with her. When I was younger I had spent a couple of Christmas holidays with Bette and my grandfather Jack before he'd passed away. They had been wonderful times for me, an escape from the realities of my mother's world to a place where I was spoilt and safe. I looked at Bette, thinking of those memories with fondness, momentarily forgetting what had brought us together again this time, with both her husband and daughter and my grandfather and mother now dead.

'Bette, I was wondering if I might be able to ask you some things about Mum?'

'Yes, of course dear. But I'm not sure that I'll be able to tell you much,' she replied.

'That's okay, I'm not really sure what I want to ask,' I said truthfully. There seemed to be so many unanswered problems in my head that I was unable to create questions for.

'Well, you see dear, she didn't really talk to me very much, I'm afraid.'

'No, I know, she didn't really talk to me either ... that's why I wanted to ask,' I replied. Now that Mum was gone I suddenly wanted to know all about her. I wanted to ask the questions I had been afraid to ask while she'd been alive. But the tricky bit was that perhaps the only person capable of answering my questions was Angie herself.

I took a sip of my tea.

'How long was she sick for? ... I mean when did it all begin, because I have only known her since she was sick? I've seen pictures of her when she was well, but I only ever remember her being sick so I was wondering when it all began?' I asked in a soft and slow manner, almost swallowing my words at first but building confidence as I went.

'She was very young,' Bette said, as she began what would be a long story. She sounded more at ease talking than I had expected.

'I think Angie was first admitted to hospital when she was about seventeen. I remember that we were in New Zealand by then, and Angie had left boarding school to work as a nanny for a family in the south.

Bette's expression changed as her thoughts drifted back to those days long gone.

Mum had been born in Kenya in East Africa, where Bette and Jack had taken freehold land following World War II. She had been the last of three girls and a disappointment, representing her father's last chance to have a boy to carry on the family name. My grandparents had successfully farmed cattle and coffee in Kenya for a number of years until political instability forced them to sell up and move, which was how they ended up in New Zealand.

'I remember as clear as a bell the day when the Morrises, Angie's employers, called me to explain that they were sending her home. They said that she had become ill and that they could no longer keep her on. They didn't say anything else and I had no idea what to expect.' Bette paused to breathe deeply.

'Jack wouldn't come to meet her off the train because he was busy on the farm. I think we had asparagus then, which required a lot of work.'

Bette took another breath and I almost wanted to tell her to stop but I didn't and, anyway, I don't think she would have.

'So I went alone to the station ... Oh Damian, I just burst into tears when I saw her, I couldn't help myself. She was so thin I just couldn't believe it. My little Angie was so sick.'

Bette very gracefully dried a tear in the corner of her eye and continued. 'Jack and I had her put into hospital straight away. I mean we had no idea

what to do, no one had any idea what to do back then. It was just horrible. She was in there for a few months, I think. I would go and visit her but she didn't like it when I did. She wouldn't want to see me. It was so hard to see her like that Damian.'

I took Bette's hand in mine and we sat like that for a while not saying anything. We both understood, we had both been there, shut out, and knew there was nothing to say.

'Eventually she left. I think the hospital found her a place to work again but that didn't last very long and we soon lost contact with her.'

'Was that when she went to Europe?' I asked. There were bits of the story I felt I already knew, having been through Mum's old photo albums with her while she recounted the adventures of her life in Europe, especially the Mediterranean.

'I guess so. But like I said, we lost contact with her and really had no idea what she was doing. The next time we heard from her she was living in Australia. She was with a man who was your father, and much to our relief she was healthy and pregnant with you,' Bette continued.

'They came over to visit us in New Zealand. It was only a brief visit but Jack and I were overwhelmed to see her so happy and healthy. I honestly thought the illness was over, then ... It broke my heart, Damian, it broke my heart when she came back with you.'

Bette paused.

'Things with your father didn't go so well and not long after you were born she called us to say she was coming back to New Zealand and could Jack help her out for a place to stay. Well, Jack set her up in a little flat in Christchurch but she just did it again ... I will never understand why. It was as though she had only started eating again just to have you, and as soon as you were born she stopped again.'

Bette stopped talking. It was late and we were both tired.

'Thank you,' I said after a while. She didn't say anything. She just got up and squeezed my shoulder as she went off to her room, leaving me to sit alone with my thoughts.

***

For me, the experience and effects of living with Mum's disease had been endured in isolation and relative silence. She intentionally cut herself off from her family and ensured that any friendships were kept at a safe and superficial level. I was unaware of the impact her illness had made on her own family until after she died. Yet I still had so many unanswered questions. What happened in her life, in those lost years in Europe and the Mediterranean? What happened then that allowed her to fulfil her desire to have a child by overcoming a disease that would cripple her for the rest of her life, and ultimately kill her? For Angie to have overcome anorexia for long enough to have a child, only then to relapse, was for Bette the most heartbreaking event in her life, yet for me it seemed to be the most inspirational act of strength and love I could ever imagine. Throughout my life Angie often referred to me as her gift, or her miracle, and now it seemed that I had only come to know the full significance of her feelings after she was gone from my life. I was always aware that she would not have lived as long as she did were it not for me, were it not for the strength she derived in wanting me to have the best life I could possibly have, a life she never had.

***

The funeral service itself was brief and it lacked the grandeur of my Hollywood-instilled expectations, as it was performed in a small, square-ish, modern brick room with plastic stackable chairs. It seems strange now, but I had never discussed with my mother where she wanted to be cremated, and so the small Buderim Crematorium, in handy location across the road from the Buderim Retirement Village, seemed as good a place as any. About two dozen people attended and I recognised about half of them. I sat in the front row with Emma on one side of me and someone else on the other, though I don't remember who. There were two or three speakers. A friend of Mum's spoke about God which left me feeling slightly annoyed, my eldest cousin praised my mother for having raised such a great son, and maybe someone else spoke. I don't remember.

Many times in my life I had contemplated what words I might offer at my mother's death to those who knew her and, more importantly, to those who only thought they knew her. I had devised great speeches about the hardships she had lived through and the pain she had endured at the hands of her illness. I had desperately wanted to reveal to the world the unrelenting battle that she and I had endured every day for so many years. But I didn't say one word. Mine was a silent eulogy.

At an appropriate moment in the proceedings a mechanical device was engaged to draw the curtains over the closed coffin located at the front of the small room. It would not have been surprising to me to learn that the funeral director had purchased the curtain machine from a roller door company, as both devices emit the same ghastly clunk-and-drag sound. The absurdity of the situation was not lost on me and at one point Emma had to tell me to stop laughing. All the while the stupid machine continued to grind the curtain along its rails cutting through the mourner's collective silence like an obnoxious drunk interjecting at a wedding.

The significance of what would occur behind the curtain must have struck everyone present. When the coffin was completely hidden from view by the curtains and the machine had stopped, a kind of finality was injected into the air.

Everyone then shuffled outside and milled around, not quite knowing what to do. Those who knew each other were grouped together and whispered pleasant things quietly enough not to offend anyone. Those who were there alone stood uncomfortably isolated in little placements among the groups, probably trying to listen to what others were saying without offending anyone. Just like at any other unrehearsed but ritualised social gathering, no one quite knew when to leave, so the milling continued. When I made my way outside, someone came quickly forward to shake my hand and communicate his commiserations. Then, like magic, he excused himself and left.

Others watched the back of this brave fellow, probably a funeral veteran, as he walked away from the collective air of discomfort and into the sunlight. Soon enough a small queue had formed in front of me as others waited their turn to at last fulfil their conscionable obligation and be gone from this place of dis-ease. My old high school vice-principal turned out to be one of those people who had no one to talk to. I was honoured that he was there, especially as I hadn't invited him and to the best of my knowledge the school had no policy supporting such action. The father of one of my old school friends came to the funeral in the place of his son who was not able to attend on the day. While it seemed unimportant to me at the time, I now reflect on this gesture with a strong sense of gratitude, because my mother had been especially fond of that mate of mine. There are no words left in my head from the conversations of that dismal afternoon. If they meant something at the time, I don't remember now. Most of what was said just passed me by.

There was a kind of vacancy to the entire experience. Whether I was intentionally blocking myself from feeling anything or I was unintentionally numbed by the events as they unfolded, the end result was the same - memory of nothing. My mother had two sisters and both attended the funeral, one flying to Australia from New Zealand with her husband. Yet I have no memory of either of them being at the funeral ceremony or at the queasy wake that followed. We had drinks and nibbles at Ian and Rachel's house in the afternoon and all I remember of that event was moving outside on my own to have a cigarette and wondering if anyone would take notice of the fact that I'd taken up smoking while in the Army. My mother was gone from my life, and so it seemed was the importance to me of everyone else there. The question I struggle with now is, 'Why?' Maybe they had already departed, those people who had once played such an important role in my life, and they momentarily returned like ghosts to remind me of the things that used to be. Like the possessions in my mother's apartment, these family members and friends who had taken various active roles in my early life were now dead to me. They belonged to my life with my mother, a life that no longer existed.

***

I travelled through that non-corporeal misplaced reality for another week trying to tie up the loose ends of my mother's life with all the skill of a child learning to tie shoelaces. I was half wanting to be free from the business, and half fearful of its impending end which would result in my return to my other reality in the Army. I spent a final night in Mum's apartment, now largely empty, except for a few basic items to entitle it the status of being rented 'semi-furnished'. I sat with Jackson, my friend from school, in the lounge room overlooking the lights of other normal houses and other supposedly normal families. We lit candles for ourselves and drank beer and wine in a failing attempt to have a meaningful experience. I would have liked to cry, to have been able to look back and think that I had felt something of real emotion in that place of my mother's final resting, but not even ambience and alcohol would afford me that one small relief. In the end it was my old bedfellow, fear, which would see me through my immediate future and ultimately give me what I had so dearly wanted to gain from safety and security.

From beginning to end – from the moment of the first phone call about my mother dying to my return to the baggy khaki world of the Army – I broke down and wept only twice. Both times were in the cold and impersonal thoroughfare of the Sydney airport terminal. On the night I returned to the Army, Ian and Rachel saw me off from the little domestic demountable building that then served as the Sunshine Coast's gateway to the rest of the country and the world. I flew on my own from Maroochydore to Sydney to wait for a connecting flight to Melbourne and ultimately a car ride back to the base. Those thirty minutes waiting in Sydney, caught alone between the two worlds of my life, were overwhelmingly painful. I was gripped by an intense fear of returning to the cold un-nurturing environment of the Army where I would be expected to reveal nothing of my inner self and continue my daily soldiering as if nothing had happened while I was on compassionate leave. At the time I mistook those feelings of fear of returning to the harsh Army life as a desire to remain connected to my mother and her memory, and what scant emotions I had about losing her from my life. I phoned Ian and Rachel from another pay phone and sobbed hopelessly into the receiver about how I couldn't possibly go back. They were soaking in the warmth of a bath and answered my call on their cordless phone, speaking words of understanding and reassurance from the steamy, soap-fragranced ambience of their bathroom.

My two options could not have been more strikingly different in that moment, as I stood there in the airport with the phone to my ear, crying. I listened to my flight being called over a computerised paging system at the same time as the soft-scented voices of the only two people of any significance left in my life. If I had been able to think of a third choice – neither returning to the Army nor remaining in the shadow of my mother's death on the Sunshine Coast – I would have taken it.

***

My fear of returning to the Army was not, as I thought at the time, based on being denied an environment to grieve. My fear was about being prevented from being truly free. Until my mother died I had no idea of the impact her life and her illness had had on me. I could identify the obvious practicalities of our interdependence but it wasn't until she was actually physically gone that I fully understood that her presence in my life had been all-pervading. I yearned to be free, to begin living my own life, a life where I came first, and fear had no place in it.

Though I didn't know it at the time, I was afraid to return to the Army because I did not want to relinquish my newfound freedom. But even in hindsight, with an awareness of this, I can't honestly say whether or not I could have taken a third option at that time – neither forward to Melbourne nor back to the Sunshine Coast, but taking a new uncharted course into Sydney. I think that somehow, over the years of my life that I shared with my mother a prevailing sense of good character had been instilled in me. A certain strength of will and inner courage had found its way into my heart, and finally feeling myself equipped with these life skills, I said goodbye, put down the phone, and boarded the plane destined to deliver me to the beginning of the rest of my life.

Publisher: www.ssoa.com.au - enquiry@ssoa.com.au

For Help with Eating Disorders
If you care for a loved one with an eating disorder, or you or
someone you know needs help with an eating disorder, call the
Butterfly Foundation helpline
1800 ED HOPE / 1800 33 4673 (FREE) or email
support@thebutterflyfoundation.org.au

For Emergency Help
If you are in an emergency situation or need immediate
assistance, you can contact mental health services or
emergency services on 000.
If you need to speak to someone urgently call:
Kids Helpline 1800 55 1800 (FREE)
Lifeline 13 11 14
or Suicide Call Back Service 1300 659 467.

Author biography

Damian Cooper lives in the Blue Mountains, west of Sydney, with his wife and daughter. He is the manager of a social welfare agency providing care and support services to vulnerable and disadvantaged youth.

From the same publisher

ARCO: the legend of the blue vortex

Ferdinando Manzo

An exciting new story from first-time novelist, Ferdinando Manzo, Arco explores man's battle with the sea in an attempt to seek solace.
The story is set in two different eras: on the high seas among ancient pirates and in contemporary Europe ravaged by war. The legend of the blue vortex – a door into another world – is the central focus of both periods.

An adventure story, it also raises philosophical questions about love and the purpose of life.

Commander Arco is at the centre of the search for the blue vortex as legend has it he was the only man who ever found it. Those who follow him are drawn to re-enact the legendary search for eternal life. The narrator, devastated by the loss of his lover, tells a tale of suspense and intrigue as he attempts to recover his lost love.

Category: FICTION Magical Realism/Romance/Fantasy

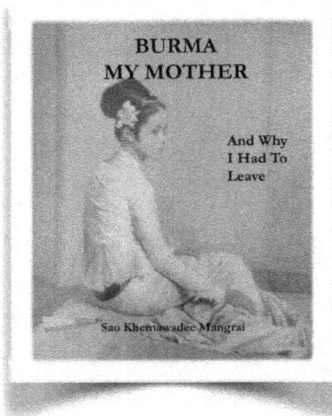

BURMA MY MOTHER And Why I Had to Leave

Sao Khemawadee Mangrai

Myanmar's future is informed by its past - and BURMA MY MOTHER tells it like it is.
A valuable story of living through good times and plenty of bad in Burma, now known as Myanmar, before an escape to a new life of freedom. The author's husband was imprisoned for 5 years, and his father was shot and killed alongside independence leader, General Aung San, when he was assassinated. Khemawadee grew up in a Shan state in the north-east of Myanmar, previously known as Burma, and now lives in Sydney.
Her sad memories are also infused by the beauty of the country and the grace of Myanmar's Buddhist culture. She also writes candidly about WWII. This book has received great praise, such as being 'unique among stories of exile', and that it is 'an extraordinary life told with clarity, gentle humour and revealing an inner strength'.
Khemawadee's memoir was written during a weekly memoir class held in Sydney, facilitated by Sydney School of Arts & Humanities.

Category: MEMOIR

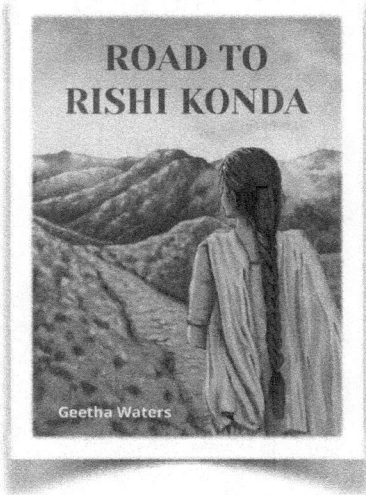

Road to Rishi Konda

Geetha Waters

'Road to Rishi Konda' by Geetha Waters is a memoir of insight and charm, with a serious educational purpose. The author recalls delightful and stimulating stories from her childhood to throw light on the work of the philosopher J. Krishnamurti as a revolutionary 20th century educator.

At once fascinating and enchanting, Geetha Waters' stories centre on a girl growing up in Kerala and Andhra Pradesh in the '60s and '70s.

These youthful tales are underpinned by Geetha's deep understanding of childhood education, based both on her academic studies and in practice in her daily life as a mother and childcare professional. Written from a child's perspective, the tales of awakening to life offer the reader an opportunity to appreciate how all children learn, as they draw on a deep well of curiosity that needs to be respected. Geetha describes how Krishnamurti would warn his students about the impact of language & conditioning, urging Geetha and her friends to observe its impact on their minds and lives.

Category: MEMOIR/BURMA-HISTORY

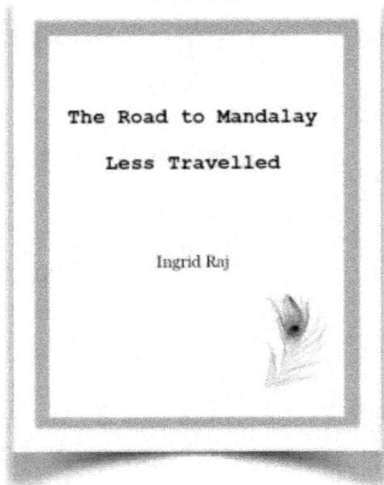

Road to Mandalay Less Travelled

Ingrid Raj

'The Road to Mandalay Less Travelled' by Ingrid Raj provides research on a selection of Anglo-Burmese writing published from the period of British rule up in Burma up until 2007. What Raj shares with us in this study is the knowledge she gained about the value of social resistance achieved through writing. Both fiction and non-fiction texts are included in arguing a case that these might be viewed as tools of often ambivalent resistance against oppressive regimes, both local and colonial.

Her research deserves a wider readership than was initially provided, and to this aim Sydney School of Arts & Humanities presents the work as its first publication in this new category of Essays & Theses. We hope that specialist researchers as well as members of the general reading public take this opportunity to learn more about the culture of the people of Myanmar through their unique approach to storytelling, based largely on their religious understanding, their rich store of folk legend and their chequered history.

Category: MEMOIR/LITERATURE/BURMA-HISTORY

Jiddu Krishnamurti World Philosopher Revised Edition

Dr C V Williams

The life of the 20th-century philosopher Jiddu Krishnamurti was truly astonishing. As this new updated edition shows, people from all over the world would gather to hear him speak the wisdom of the ages.

Biographer Christine (CV) Williams carried out research over a period of four years to write this ebook account of Krishnamurti's life. She studied his major archive of personal correspondence and talks, and interviewed people who knew him intimately.

Krishna was born into poverty in a South Indian village, before being adopted by a wealthy English public figure, Annie Besant. As an adult he settled in California, travelling to India and England every year to give public lectures that inspired spiritual seekers beyond any single religion.

Category: BIOGRAPHY

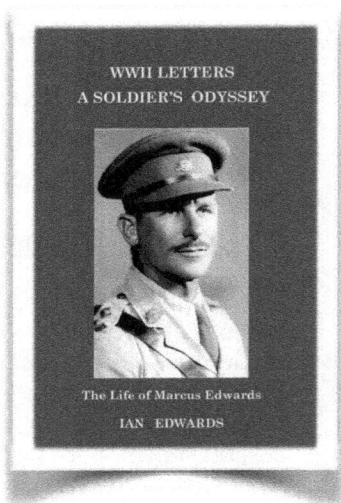

The Life of Marcus Edwards

by Ian Edwards

This biography of Marcus Edwards is an astonishing chronicle of the life of a soldier on the WWII frontline Written by Marcus Edwards' nephew, Ian Edwards, the work draws largely on the soldier's correspondence and diary notes from the Second World War in particular. The letters provide revelations about conditions of living in the major war zones of Europe and North Africa.

Edwards enlisted as a gunner soon after the declaration of war in 1939, and fought on several fronts in the 2/2 Field Regiment of the Royal Australian Artillery before being taken prisoner in 1941.

After a successful campaign against Italian forces at Bardia and then Tobruk, Marcus saw action in Greece before his regiment was evacuated to Crete in 1941. He was captured there in June 1941 and transported to Germany as a prisoner of war, from where he was released in 1945.

His description of his last days in the combat zone of Greece is shocking, as he and his mates faced a barrage of German dive-bombing and machine-gunning.

'They came over in massed waves, one after the other. Their casualties must have been colossal and still our men held them … Their tanks, again in masses, made our one armoured division look laughable. You see, we had neither the men nor the equipment,' he wrote.

Category: BIOGRAPHY